CHESS IN TEN LESSONS

by LARRY EVANS

Chess is a fine art—but it requires no exceptional scientific or mathematical ability.

This book, by an acknowledged chess genius, assumes that the student knows absolutely nothing about chess and leads him to the point where he can conduct an intelligent game. It is a complete, practical, modern presentation of the "royal" game. The, visual approach, using 183 diagrams, enables anyone to learn at a glance.

Larry Evans is a Grandmaster, the highest title that can be awarded by the International Chess Federation. All his knowledge and experience have gone into the creation of this work which not only provides a clear exposition of basic principles but also countless tips for the novice as well as the more advanced player. The questions of what to do, what not to do, and why are answered fully in text and diagrams. Much space is devoted to particularly knotty problems and exercises.

Although no book can turn anyone into an expert by magic, this volume makes it possible for the student—even if he is completely unfamiliar with chess—to become a proficient player if he has the will to learn.

A wise man once wrote: "Chess, like love, like music, has the power to make man happy." The reader will discover this for himself. After studying **Chess in Ten Lessons,** the reader will find that he need no longer miss out on the fun of playing this "king" of indoor sports.

CHESS IN TEN LESSONS

Contents

Lesson 1. How the Pieces Move

Lesson 2. What the Pieces Are Worth

Lesson 3. How to Read Chess Notation

Lesson 4. Drawn Games

Lesson 5. The King Hunt

Lesson 6. The Endgame

Lesson 7. The Opening

Lesson 8. Winning Tactics

Lesson 9. Exercises in Combination Play

Lesson 10. Game Section

Appendix. The Official Laws of Chess

CHESS

in ten lessons

by

Larry Evans
International Grandmaster

Melvin Powers
WILSHIRE BOOK COMPANY
12015 Sherman Road
No. Hollywood, California 91605

Library of Congress Catalog Card Number: 59-12208

Printed in the United States of America

Other Books by Larry Evans

Vienna International Tournament, 1922
David Bronstein's Best Chess Games, 1944-1949
Championship Chess and Checkers for All (with Tom Wiswell)
Trophy Chess (First Rosenwald Trophy Tournament, 1954-55)
New Ideas in Chess

ISBN 0-87980-015-1

CONTENTS

		Page
Lesson 1	**HOW THE PIECES MOVE**	9
	Rules	9
	The King	12
	The Rook	14
	The Bishop	15
	The Queen	16
	The Knight	18
	The Pawn	20
	En passant capturing	22
	Pawn promotion	23
	Castling	24
Lesson 2	**WHAT THE PIECES ARE WORTH**	26
	Table of Comparative Values	26
	Illustrative Diagrams	27
Lesson 3	**HOW TO READ CHESS NOTATION**	29
	Master Chart	30
	Chess Movies	30
	Other Abbreviations	35
Lesson 4	**DRAWN GAMES**	36
	5 Ways to Draw	36
Lesson 5	**THE KING HUNT**	40
	24 Problems	40
	Solutions	53

Lesson 6 THE ENDGAME **55**
  Endings Without Pawns on the Board 55
    King and Queen vs. King 56
    King and Rook vs. King 57
    King and Two Bishops vs. King 58
    King, Bishop and Knight vs. King 59
  Endings With Pawns on the Board 62
    King and Queen vs. King and Pawn 62
    King and Pawn vs. King 65

Lesson 7 THE OPENING **69**
  The Center and Development 69
  Sample Opening (Giuoco Piano) 71
  General Principles 73
  The First Move 74
  King Pawn Openings (chart) 75
  Queen Pawn Openings (chart) 78
  Ten Tricks and Traps 80

Lesson 8 WINNING TACTICS **83**
  Discovered Attack 83
  Double Check 84
  Forking Attacks 85
  Pinning Attacks 86
  Deflecting Maneuvers 87
  X-Ray Attacks 89
  20 Exercises 89
  Solutions 100

Lesson 9 EXERCISES IN COMBINATION PLAY **102**
  60 Problems 103
  Solutions 118

Lesson 10 GAME SECTION **124**
  15 Tournament Games 124

Appendix THE OFFICIAL LAWS OF CHESS **183**

LESSON 1
HOW THE PIECES MOVE

Diagram 1

The chessboard — battlefield royal!

Chess is an ancient game of skill involving two opponents. It also may be played in consultation, with two or more persons on each team. The battlefield consists of 64 squares, all of which are used. Whatever the actual color of your board and chessmen (some are green and buff, others red and black) it is customary to refer to the 32 light squares as WHITE and to the 32 dark ones as BLACK. Note that the board is always placed with a white square at the lower right hand corner of each player (arrow).

Each player has 16 men. Like a good general, each is expected to guard this MATERIAL and never sacrifice a man without good reason. In the diagrams used throughout this book the following figures represent the chessmen.

9

The Chessmen

—1 King—

—1 Queen—

—2 Bishops—

—2 Knights—

—2 Rooks—

—8 Pawns—

White army   *Black army*

Unlike card games which feature the "luck of the draw," each chess contest starts from the same position. Yet — with rare exceptions — two games are never exactly identical. Here is the way the pieces are always set up at the beginning of every game. Memorize this lineup and/or refer to it when you start play.

The King and Queen pose proudly in the center of this family portrait, surrounded by their children (the Pawns) and the royal retinue. The Queen always goes "on her own color" (White Queen on white, Black Queen on black) — a remnant of feudal gallantry to ladies. Next come the Bishops, then the Knights, then the Rooks. These important pieces are arrayed along the FIRST RANK. The 8 Pawns are arranged for protection along the SECOND RANK. A "rank" is simply a row of 8 horizontal squares.

Q. How many ranks are on the chessboard? A. 8.

WHITE ALWAYS MOVES FIRST. Each player continues moving alternately until the game is over. Under no circumstances may one side "pass" or make two moves in a row. (In all

Diagram 2

The starting lineup.

our diagrams White moves "up" the board and Black is coming "down" — toward him.)

THE OBJECT OF THE GAME IS TO CHECKMATE THE ENEMY KING. When the King is trapped and ready to be captured (the King is never *actually* captured) you call out "checkmate" and it's all over. Checkmate is unlikely early in the battle, so you should try to wear down your opponent by winning his material. If neither player can gain any advantage, and all the pieces are evenly swapped, the game is likely to terminate in a DRAW or tie.

IT IS NECESSARY TO MEMORIZE THE POWERS OF EACH MAN AND WHAT HE IS WORTH IN RELATION TO THE OTHER CHESSMEN. By studying the following diagrams anyone can master these simple, clear-cut rules in a matter of minutes.

1. PIECES MAY MOVE IN ONLY ONE DIRECTION AT A TIME, LANDING ON UNOCCUPIED SQUARES (EXCEPT WHEN MAKING CAPTURES). WITH THE EXCEPTION OF THE KNIGHT'S LEAP, NO MAN MAY

PASS OR JUMP OVER A PIECE WHICH IS IN ITS
PATH.

2. CAPTURES ARE MADE BY REMOVING THE ENEMY
PIECE FROM THE BOARD AND OCCUPYING ITS
SQUARE WITH THE CAPTURING MAN. ALL CAP-
TURES ARE *OPTIONAL*.

3. NO MOVE MAY EVER BE MADE WHICH LEAVES
THE KING IN, OR EXPOSES IT TO, CAPTURE OR
CHECK. IF A PLAYER MAKES A MOVE AND OVER-
LOOKS THAT HIS KING IS ATTACKED, HIS OPPO-
NENT MUST CALL THIS TO HIS ATTENTION AND
PERMIT HIM TO TAKE HIS LAST MOVE BACK IN
ORDER TO SAFEGUARD THE KING.

THE KING

Diagram 3

The King moves one square in any direction.

If you lose your King, you lose the game! Guard him carefully.
In the early days, when the game was played in Persia, the King
was known as the "Shah." When the Shah was captured the
players said "Shah-mat!" — the King is dead! The other pieces
help to protect the King.

How does the King capture? He captures in the same way he moves. But remember: no piece is compelled to capture an enemy man (as in checkers).

Diagram 4

"A" — before the King captures the Rook.
"B" — after the Rook has been taken.

The Black Rook is used for purposes of illustration only. The King may capture any enemy unit provided that he does not expose himself to check (see rule 3).

Study the King on your own set carefully. Its shape gives a clue to how it moves. The cross protruding from the top means the King may *cross in any direction:* backwards, forwards, sideways, diagonally — the equivalent of "beating a strategic retreat in actual warfare.

Q. How many squares can the Rook stop at in diagram 5? *A. 14.* Again, the shape of the Rook on your own set provides the key to its move. Notice the four notches in its tower. This means that the Rook can move in *4 different directions.*

Q. How does the Rook capture? *A. As it moves.* Q. What can the Rook capture? *A. Any enemy unit along its path.*

THE ROOK

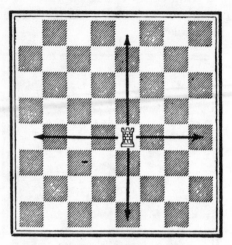

Diagram 5

The Rook moves north, south, east or west any desired number of squares, provided there is nothing obstructing its path.

Diagram 6

"A" — the Rook may capture the Knight OR
"B" — the Rook may capture the Pawn.

The Rook is not compelled to capture either piece, nor may it take both of them in the same move. Like the King, and all the other pieces, the Rook must capture and then rest after gorging itself.

The word "rook" is believed to have been derived from the Arabs, who spoke of a mythical two-headed bird that was capable of carrying an elephant in its claws. That bird was a *rukh*, from which comes our English word rook for the blackbird.

THE BISHOP

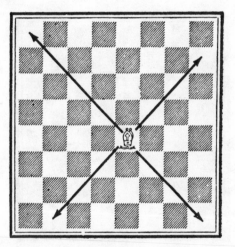

Diagram 7

The Bishop may move in diagonal lines any desired number of squares, but it cannot zigzag.

The Bishop is the man with the split cap, and this reminds us that he moves via the slashing diagonals. A Bishop may move in only one direction at a time in straight lines, and he is forever limited to squares of the same color. But turn back to diagram 2 and you will observe that each side has *two* Bishops in the starting lineup. One of them must stay on black and the other on white squares.

Q. In diagram 7 how many squares may the Bishop stop at?
A. *13.* (Follow the arrows and count each square en route.)

The Bishop was originally called an elephant, and the un-
limited diagonal move was introduced in the 16th century when
the power of most of the major pieces was altered. Europe preferred to think of chess as a replica of the court rather than an
image of warfare. Accordingly, the French named this piece *le
fou* — the jester — and made him a member of the royal retinue.
The English designated this piece the Bishop because the two
projections at the top (supposed to represent elephant tusks)
resembled a mitre.

THE QUEEN

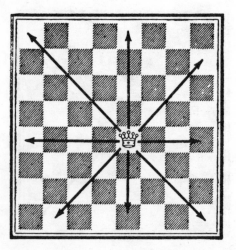

Diagram 8

**The Queen moves north, south, east or west (like a Rook)
or diagonally (like a Bishop).**

The Queen (which combines the powers of Rook *and* Bishop)
is the most powerful piece. Q. How many squares can the Queen
stop at in diagram 8? A. 27.

This gives some idea of the relationship between the men.
Here White is a Queen ahead — an overwhelming material advantage — and Black's royal majesty is trapped in a pigsty.

Q. Why is Black checkmated if White moves his Queen to any
one of the 4 squares indicated? A. *Because Black's King is at-*

Diagram 9

If the Queen moves to one of the 4 squares indicated by the arrows, White calls out checkmate and that's the end of the ball game!

tacked and he cannot get out of check without being captured. ("Check" means the King is attacked!) *The Black King can take the Queen on squares 1 and 2, but this is illegal because White's King would get him in turn.*

Q. Why wouldn't Black be checkmated even if White didn't move his Queen to one of the indicated squares? A. *Because in order to checkmate the enemy King you have to attack him: threaten to capture him with your next move. Only the Queen to one of these 4 squares leaves Black no escape. Any other move would be sloppy, although White could still win.*

A PLAYER IS CHECKMATED WHEN HE CANNOT (A) BLOCK THE CHECK BY PUTTING A MAN IN THE WAY — THIS IS KNOWN AS "INTERPOSITION"; (B) CAPTURE THE CHECKING PIECE; (C) MOVE HIS KING OUT OF CHECK TO A SAFE SQUARE WHERE IT IS NOT STILL SUBJECT TO CAPTURE.

The Queen's crown has 8 points, indicating that it may move in any of 8 different directions. The Queen is the second largest piece (next to the King) and, like most women, is the power behind the throne. She has more freedom of movement than any other piece.

In Persia, before chess was known in Europe, the Queen was a masculine piece called the "Farzin," the Counselor. It could only step one square in any direction (like the King moves today) and its duty was to advise and defend his royal majesty.

In the 15th or 16th century the Queen changed sex and was emancipated. Its growth in power and mobility probably paralleled the rising importance of women historically. There is no Queen in Chinese chess even today because of the low esteem with which females were held in the Orient!

THE KNIGHT

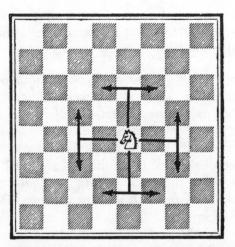

Diagram 10

The Knight is the only piece which does not move in a straight line. He leaps 2 squares in any direction and then sidesteps one, to form a right angle.

The Knight always moves 3 squares away in a L-shape. If it starts on a white square, it must land on a black square; if it starts on black, then it must end on white.

Another way to describe the Knight's move is: he leaps two squares left or right, and then one square up or down. He is the only man that can literally "jump" over friendly or enemy units, like a horse clearing a hurdle.

Q. In diagram 10, how many squares can the Knight move to? A. 8. Of course the Knight may only leap to unoccupied squares (*except* when capturing). It may *not* capture any piece which it jumps over. It captures within striking distance when it lands, and in this respect is similar to all the other men. Q. How does the Knight capture? A. *As it moves, see in diagram 11*

Diagram 11

"A" — **Knight may capture the Queen OR Rook.**
"B" — **Knight has captured the Queen.**

The Knight has decided to take the Queen because it is the more valuable of the two enemy units.

The double attack pictured in diagram 11 is known as a KNIGHT FORK. One way to master the tricky gyration of the Knight is to study its shape on your own set. From his nose to the tip of his ear forms a right angle.

The Knight is equivalent to the cavalry of the chessboard. He is the brave, prancing charger always found in the heat of battle.

Its basic move has remained the same for over thirteen centuries. In medieval Europe, however, its name was changed from horse to Knight.

THE PAWN

Diagram 12

The Pawn can never retreat! He marches straight forward — one space at a time.

Every Pawn if it wishes can move forward two squares on his first move (in the starting lineup) provided that both spaces are vacant. The Pawn is the foot soldier, the plodding infantry man who clears the way for the other pieces. Like any soldier, he can kill!

The Pawn is unique in two respects: (1) it is the only man that can never retreat; (2) it does NOT capture as it moves (see diagram 13). It captures *diagonally* — not straight.

This double attack is an example of a PAWN FORK. If White decided to capture one of the enemy units, the Pawn would carry out the order by removing it from the board and occupying its square. The Pawn's power to capture consists of its V-shaped prong.

Q. In 14A, if it were White's move, why couldn't his Pawn

Diagram 13

The Pawn captures diagonally, straight ahead. In this example it may take either the Rook or the Knight.

Diagram 14

"A" — both Pawns are blocked.
"B" — White has just captured a Black piece.
"C" — the Pawn's path is blocked by the Queen.

simply capture Black's Pawn? A. *Because a Pawn cannot capture straight ahead, only diagonally. Neither Pawn is free to advance here; there is no enemy for either one to capture.*

Q. If it were White's move in 14B, could his Pawn capture Black's Pawn? A. *No, Pawns capture diagonally straight ahead — not sideways. Both Pawns, however, are now free to advance.*

Q. In 14C, if it were White's move, could he advance his Pawn? A. *No, the Pawn is immobile. It cannot advance diagonally because there is nothing for it to capture. It cannot march straight ahead until the Queen is moved out of the way.*

Diagram 15

"A" — White's Pawn uses its initial double move.
"B" — Black captures en passant ("in passing"), AS IF White had advanced only one space.

Pawns may capture other Pawns ONLY in this special situation, known as capturing EN PASSANT. If a player does not exercise his privilege at the first opportunity (on his very next move) he loses it, and the position stands.

When a Pawn stands on the FIFTH RANK (5 rows forward) it may capture an enemy Pawn which "passes" on an adjacent FILE (the 8 *vertical* rows are called "files").

Only Pawns can capture in this fashion. It does not apply to the other men. Incidentally, this rule was not always in effect. When the Pawn was granted the initial double move (circa 1560) many players objected that this cheated them of the right to take an enemy Pawn, which would normally have happened. *En passant* was adopted as a compromise to meet this objection. The Pawn captures obliquely, for one thing, because the soldier used to kill by a sidewards thrust of his sword.

For a common soldier, the Pawn is capable of many surprises. But here is the biggest surprise of all: *the Pawn is a prince in disguise!* If he succeeds in reaching the last row, known as the EIGHTH RANK, he can become any piece you want to make him — Queen, Rook, Bishop or Knight — even if you still have your original pieces. This is called PAWN PROMOTION. Changing him with this magic wand to anything less than a Queen is called UNDERPROMOTION, but this is generally not done without some good reason. (If one Queen is already on the board, a Rook is generally turned upside down to indicate a second one.)

Diagram 16

"A" — the Pawn is about to be crowned.
"B" — the Pawn has been queened.

Notice that a Queen has been substituted for the Pawn, which has now shed its beggar's garments. The Queen's new power takes effect *immediately*. The Pawn's lowly origin is completely forgotten.

There is only one other special rule you need to know before getting started: CASTLING. This movement involves the King and the Rook at the same time. EACH PLAYER MAY CASTLE ONCE EVERY GAME PROVIDED THE FOLLOWING RULES ARE OBSERVED.

Diagram 17A

Position before castling.

Diagram 17B

Position after the King castles K-side.

Diagram 17C

Position after the King castles Q-side.

The King shifts two squares to the right or left and the Rook tucks him in. The purpose of this movement is to bring the King to safety and the Rook into play. Which wing the King chooses depends on the protection he is afforded once he gets there.

1. In order to castle, the squares intervening between the

King and the Rook which is to be used must be vacant. 2. Neither the King nor the Rook may have previously moved (or the privilege is forfeited). 3. The King cannot castle out of, through, or into check.

Mobile towers were popular war machines in the Middle Ages; these were constructed of wood and mounted on rollers or wheels. One can easily picture his majesty retiring into one of these rolling fortresses for his own protection. The custom eventually found its way into chess, whose rules very often reflect the era in which the game was born.

YOU NOW KNOW ALL THE RULES OF CHESS AND ARE READY TO PLAY YOUR FIRST GAME. WHAT TO DO, WHAT NOT TO DO, AND SOME FINE POINTS ARE EXPLAINED IN THE FOLLOWING LESSONS.

LESSON 2
WHAT THE PIECES ARE WORTH

During the course of battle, pieces are constantly being exchanged. Each player must make sure always to get his money's worth or better. Here is a yardstick by which to judge whether you are ahead or behind in material. MEMORIZE this table.

Table of Comparative Values

Pawn = 1 unit (buck private)
Knight = 3 units (2nd lieutenant)
Bishop = 3 units (1st lieutenant)
Rook = 5 units (major)
Queen = 10 units (general)

The King is equivalent to the commander-in-chief. He has no commodity value because Kings cannot be swapped: once checkmate occurs, the game is over.

This table is relative. The power of a piece depends upon its post in any given position. In general, the more mobility the piece has, the more powerful it is.

Obviously a Pawn on the 7th rank which cannot be prevented from queening is worth infinitely more than a mere Pawn under normal circumstances. The important thing to remember is that it is foolhardy to give up a man needlessly without *full* compensation.

Q. How many Rooks = 1 Queen? A. *2 Rooks (5+5=10 units).*

Q. How many Pawns = 1 Bishop? A. *3 Pawns (1+1+1=3 units).*

A player who succeeds in winning his opponent's Rook for a Bishop or Knight is said to have gained "the exchange," or "the quality," as it is sometimes called.

THE PLAYER WHO IS AHEAD IN MATERIAL IS WELL ON THE ROAD TO VICTORY. The winning technique consists of swapping down to the elementary endgames analyzed in lesson 4.

In order to size up a position simply count heads and "pair off." It is always necessary to consider your opponent's reply when planning your move. Whenever he makes a play, ask yourself: "WHAT IS THE OBJECT OF HIS MOVE?"

Here are a few positions which illustrate the principle of capture and recapture.

Diagram 18

White is momentarily a Pawn ahead (count men!) but Black can even things up by recapturing with his Pawn (see arrow). Go on to Diagram 19.

Diagram 19

This is the way the position now looks. It would be a mistake for White to play Knight takes Pawn because then Black's Queen would get the Knight.

Diagram 20

Suppose Black had made the mistake of starting with Queen takes Pawn. What would White do now? He has a good move staring him in the face! (See Diagram 21.)

Diagram 21

Naturally White snatches the Queen with his Knight! True, Black can now play Pawn takes Knight. But White still comes out 7 units ahead. (Subtract 3 for the Knight from 10 for the Queen.)

LESSON 3
HOW TO READ CHESS NOTATION

Notation is merely a method of recording chess games. By means of this shorthand, games which are hundreds of years old can be replayed and enjoyed today. It is not necessary to know notation in order to play chess; but you must learn it if you want to study chess books.

Other than serving as the medium for transmitting moves to you, these numbers and abbreviations have no special significance. In lesson two we wrote moves out in longhand. In diagram 21, for instance, we described a move by "Pawn takes Knight." In chess notation this would read, PxN. ("N" is used rather than "Kt" in modern notation.) Each piece is abbreviated by using its first initial, as follows:

Piece	Symbol
King (K)	
Queen (Q)	
Rook (R)	
Bishop (B)	
Knight (N)	
Pawn (P)	

Thus QP means "Queen Pawn," the Pawn which stands on the Queen file. A file, as you remember, is a row of 8 vertical squares. There are 8 files, and these are named after the pieces which occupy the first ranks in the original lineup.

Thus KB means "King Bishop," the one which originally stands closest to the King. QR similarly means "Queen Rook," the one which is housed nearest to the Queen.

Q. What does QRP mean? *A. Queen Rook Pawn.*
Q. What does KNP mean? *A. King Knight Pawn.*

Diagram 22　　　　　MASTER CHART

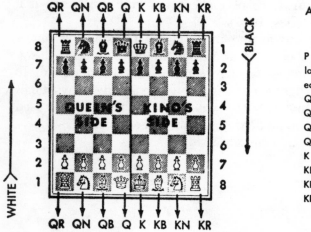

ABBREVIATIONS

P = Pawn (though not labeled in this diagram, each side has 8 Pawns)
QR = Queen's Rook
QN = Queen's Knight
QB = Queen's Bishop
Q = Queen
K = King
KB = King's Bishop
KN = King's Knight
KR = King's Rook

The numbers refer to the ranks. Each player measures a move from *his* side of the board. He counts forward. If White starts the game by advancing his King Pawn two squares this is written as "1 P—K4." (Pawn to King four.) We don't have to specify which Pawn, because the KP is the only one which can go to K4.

How about Black? He follows the same system, counting forward from *his* side. K4 from White's side of the board is K5 from Black's point-of-view. If Black starts by advancing his KP two squares, we describe that move as "1 ... P—K4." (The 3 dots in front of the move indicate that it is a Black move.)

Here is a chess movie featuring the Scholar's Mate, one of

the oldest opening traps. Simply follow the diagrams in order, from 23 to 29. Set up the position on your own board in order to get the feel of the chessmen.

Diagram 23

White has opened the game with 1 P—K4. The dash obviously indicates "to." It separates the piece which moves from the square to which it moves.

Diagram 24

Black counters with the routine 1 . . . P—K4 (indicated by the arrow). This move frees the Queen and the Bishop for action.

Diagram 25

White continues 2 B—B4, developing a piece and focusing on Black's weakest square — his KB2.

Diagram 26

And Black, in his turn, makes a healthy developing move, 2 . . . B—B4. Notice that 2 . . . B—(Q)B4 is not written because there is only one "B4" square that the Bishop can go to.

Diagram 27

White hazards 3 Q—R5, threatening to capture Black's KP (King Pawn) and KBP. Ordinarily the Queen should not move in the opening, for it is likely to lose time when it is driven back. Here, however, it pays dividends . . .

Diagram 28

. . . for Black makes his first blunder: 3 . . . P—Q3?, protecting the KP but overlooking White's retort. The correct move is 3 . . . Q—K2 which defends everything.

Diagram 29

White plays 4 Q x P checkmate — the game is over! The Black King has no legal move on the board (try all his moves and see!) and he cannot capture the Queen since it is defended by the Bishop. White's Queen attacks the King diagonally.

Let us now review the full score of the game up to this point. Here is how it would look when printed in columns. The moves are read *across* the columns, from left to right. After move 1 has been made for both sides, then move down to move 2 and repeat this procedure until the game is over. For every White move there must be a corresponding reply by Black.

White	Black
1 P—K4	P—K4
2 B—B4	B—B4
3 Q—R5	P—Q3?
4 Q x BP mate	

Here is another way of recording these same moves in order to save space. This method is generally used when annotating or commenting upon the moves made in the column: 1 P—K4, P—K4; 2 B—B4, B—B4; 3 Q—R5, P—Q3?; 4 Q x BP mate.

Still another way of recording these same moves is in a column, straight down the page, with White's move above the line and Black's reply below it. This method is used in manuals on the opening which are crowded and crammed with variations and sub-variations.

1 <u>P—K4</u>
   P—K4
2 <u>B—B4</u>
   B—B4
3 <u>Q—R5</u>
   P—Q3?
4 Q x BP mate

Other Abbreviations

<u>O—O</u>	=	castles K-side
<u>O—O—O</u>	=	castles Q-side
e.p.	=	captures *en passant*
ch or <u>+</u>	=	check
dbl. ch or <u>++</u>	=	double check
<u>dis. ch.</u>	=	discovered check
<u>!</u>	=	star move
<u>?</u>	=	mistake

LESSON 4
DRAWN GAMES

Not every game ends in victory. Many of them result in hard-fought draws. Since every game starts with equal forces, one would most games to end in a tie. But because chess is a game of skill *par excellence,* the better player invariably wins.

Let us review the ways in which games may be tied. (See also "The Laws of Chess" in the appendix.)

1. **By mutual agreement,** when neither player feels he has any advantage. In tournaments, this is the most common method of drawing. Beginners, however, are advised to play each game out to the bitter end — the last mistake loses!

2. **When the same position repeats itself three times,** consecutively or not. In order to prove this in tournament games, a player must submit his score-sheet to the referee and claim a draw by repetition.

3. **The 50 move rule.** If a player can prove that no capture or Pawn push has occurred in the last 50 moves. This rule penalizes lack of skill and is only invoked under special circumstances in the endgame, when one side has a considerable material advantage and does not know how to make any progress.

4. **When there is not enough material left on the board to force checkmate,** despite how strongly one side desires to win. This case of matter over mind is known as a "technical draw." For one example, see diagram 30.

In order to win, White would need a second Bishop or a Knight or a Pawn (in order to promote it to a new Queen). He has no piece which controls the dark squares, and Kings cannot approach within one square of each other. (The Kings in diagram 30 can come no closer — a no man's land separates them. They are said to be in "opposition.")

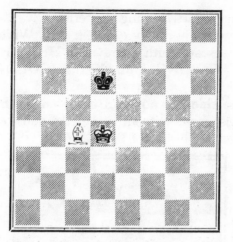

Diagram 30

White is a Bishop ahead but he cannot win, even against inferior defense. A technical draw.

5. When one player can administer an endless series of checks, while his opponent is unable to put a stop to them. This is known as PERPETUAL CHECK.

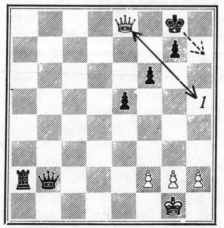

Diagram 31

White's Queen administers perpetual check by following the arrow to 1 and back again. The King has no choice but to move back and forth.

Black has an overwhelming material advantage (he is a Rook up) and would normally expect to win. White is naturally very happy to "escape with a draw." WHEN THERE IS NO CHANCE OF WINNING, A PLAYER SHOULD FIGHT FOR THE DRAW.

6. **When one side has no legal move on the board** and his King cannot move without being captured (but it is not in check either). This is a STALEMATE.

Diagram 32

White (on move) is stalemated — draw!

Again, Black has an overwhelming material advantage — but White has no legal move and his King is NOT in check. Notice that all the Pawns are blocked.

Q. If it were Black's move now, he has 3 ways to administer checkmate in one move. What are these ways? *A. 1 . . . Q—B6 mate OR 1 . . . Q—N8 mate OR 1 . . . B—N8 discovered mate (the Rook unmasks an attack on White's King).*

Diagram 33 is a position which White would also normally expect to win. He is a Rook, Bishop, and Pawn ahead (determine this for yourself by counting pieces on the board). If it were White's move, **1 Q—Q6+** would lead to a handy win. Black would be forced to move his King and White would follow-up with another check. But because it is now Black's move he has a tactic — a swindling resource — which permits him to escape with a draw by stalemate. *Deus ex machina!*

Diagram 33

Black (on move) can draw by sacrificing his Queen (see arrow)! This leads to stalemate.

The solution is **1 ... Q—K3!!+**. White cannot ignore the check and must play **2 Q x Q** (any other move would permit Black to capture White's Queen for nothing), whereupon it is STALEMATE — Black has no legal move and his King is NOT in check. This requires alertness and ingenuity. Black must see the final position in his mind's eye before embarking on the COMBINATION.

Briefly, let us review *checkmate, check, and stalemate*.

CHECKMATE means the King is directly attacked and has no way to get out.

CHECK means the King is attacked, but there is a way to get out. A check by itself, without any follow-up, generally is harmless.

STALEMATE means the King is *not* attacked; moreover, there is no legal move on the board with the King or any other man — Draw game.

LESSON 5
THE KING HUNT

Sound the horns! Unleash the hounds! You are all invited to join in the King hunt.

The most important term in chess, certainly the most melancholy for the loser, is *checkmate*. Learning how to recognize this situation calls for alertness and ability. This exercise is designed to help you.

Here are 24 TEASERS to sharpen your eye. Throw everything you have at the enemy King. Don't be detoured or sidetracked. No matter how impossible it looks, you have the advantage of knowing that a mate is in the air. These problems are all taken from actual games. In most of them, the side which is on move will be behind in material because heavy sacrifices were incurred to arrive at these favorable settings. You are required only to find the finishing touch.

THERE IS ONE AND ONLY ONE SOLUTION TO EACH PROBLEM. Try to solve directly from the diagrams. If you have time, set up each position on your own board. Do not touch the chessmen in working it out. Try to solve in your mind, visualizing the pieces as they change positions. Use the process of elimination. If a move merely gives check and the enemy King has a momentary escape — even if he can forestall mate by one move — then you are on the wrong track.

A chessmaster can solve any of these problems in a split second, merely by glancing at the diagram. The beginner, however, necessarily must get oriented. Do not be discouraged if you are stumped. And take as much time as you need. Accuracy is more important than speed.

Notice carefully whether White or Black is on move. Diagrams 54 to 57 feature mate in TWO moves. The solutions follow diagram 57.

Diagram 34

WHITE MATES IN 1 MOVE
Does his majesty feel a draft? Black's King is exposed — his K-side Pawn structure has been shattered by a Queen sacrifice. Now comes the finishing touch.

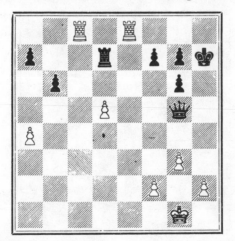

Diagram 35

WHITE MATES IN 1 MOVE
Just turn the key — it fits the lock! In order to enforce checkmate, you have to attack the enemy King. This is the tail end of a combination — White gave up his Queen to enjoy this last chuckle.

Diagram 36

WHITE MATES IN 1 MOVE
The Pawn is a chameleon! Here, again, White is decisively
behind in material. If you're stuck, refer back to the section on Pawn promotion. Enough said!

Diagram 37

WHITE MATES IN 1 MOVE
Many checks — but only one doesn't bounce! From an em-
barrassment of riches White must select one bonbon —
not boo-boo.

Diagram 38

WHITE MATES IN 1 MOVE
Black's King is in a mousetrap! Who knows what is concealed beneath a crown? Even the mighty can be brought low.

Diagram 39

WHITE MATES IN 1 MOVE
Necessity is the mother of invention! White is a Queen and a Rook behind. He hasn't got many pieces which can attack Black's King. But one is more than enough — if its tone is right.

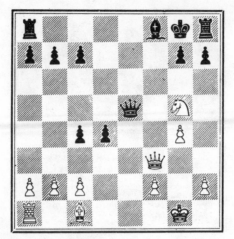

Diagram 40

WHITE MATES IN 1 MOVE
Invade! Invade! Invade! Don't dally. Cross the Maginot
line and bring back the Kaiser.

Diagram 41

WHITE MATES IN 1 MOVE
Come on in — the water's fine! Take the plunge. If you
know how to dive, you won't hit rock bottom — but pay
dirt instead.

Diagram 42

WHITE MATES IN 1 MOVE
Black has bottled himself up! The corkscrew is at hand. Pop goes the monarch!

Diagram 43

WHITE MATES IN 1 MOVE
If Columbus discovered America, you can discover this, mates! Steer north by east. The wind blows from 2 directions — double check.

Diagram 44

WHITE MATES IN 1 MOVE
Strike while the iron is hot! Or at least White had better offer some excuse for just having lost his Queen.

Diagram 45

WHITE MATES IN 1 MOVE
They also serve who stand and wait! A bayonet will have to do when the cannons are gone. A King is never safe around a battlefield.

Diagram 46

WHITE MATES IN 1 MOVE

Black's King is caught like a rat in a tunnel! He has no air-space. Flush him out. Extermination is the chessplayer's first duty.

Diagram 47

WHITE MATES IN 1 MOVE

Queen and Bishop — lots of mischief. It's the season — rhyme and reason. Well, bad poets often make good chessplayers.

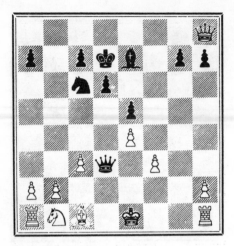

Diagram 48

BLACK MATES IN 1 MOVE

Bring up the reserves! Alas! While White's Queen has taken a vacation and feasted on Black's Rooks, a dastardly plot has been hatched.

Diagram 49

BLACK MATES IN 1 MOVE

An open file and a Rook to steer her by! Black hasn't got his Queen left, so he's entitled to take a little poetic license.

Diagram 50

BLACK MATES IN 1 MOVE
It's a dark night! His majesty can easily get lost in the moor. Ah! Such an unloved King to be without friends, at an hour like this.

Diagram 51

BLACK MATES IN 1 MOVE
Beware the optical illusion! Black is a Bishop behind and what has he to show for it? Not even a good check. But a mate without a check is like a pearl without an oyster. Stop talking in riddles! This is a serious affair.

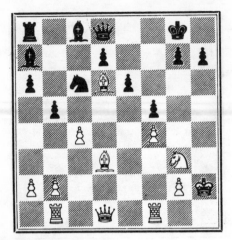

Diagram 52

BLACK MATES IN 1 MOVE

Always check — it may be mate! This is an old saw —
see to it that you get the point. Seesaw. Get it?

Diagram 53

BLACK MATES IN 1 MOVE

White is a pin-cushion! Now what in the world do we
mean by that? Just remember that no move may be
made which exposes the King to capture. More confused
than ever? Good.

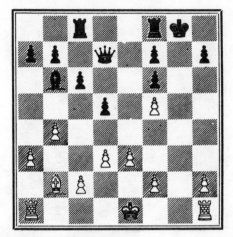

Diagram 54

WHITE MATES IN 2 MOVES
The 1-2 punch! It is exhausting to keep punching with
the same hand. White had better hit hard because he's
a Queen behind.

Diagram 55

WHITE MATES IN 2 MOVES
Smothered mate! A neat pirouette with the lady forces
Black to seal his own casket — and there is no way out
forever after. This is one of the most beautiful themes in
chess.

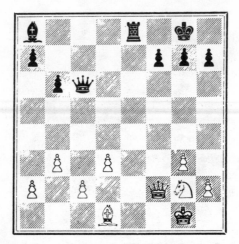

Diagram 56

BLACK MATES IN 2 MOVES

It is better to give than to receive! With some players it's Xmas the year round. But perhaps they have some ulterior motives. We always suspect generosity.

Diagram 57

BLACK MATES IN 2 MOVES

Give till it hurts — White! Maybe this is cynical. Since this is the last teaser, here is an easy sop.

SOLUTIONS

34 1 R—N3 mate. White exploits the open KN file to launch a final attack.

35 1 R—R8 mate. Notice that there is no need to specify 1 R—(K)R8.

36 P—N8=Q mate. This is a splendid illustration of Pawn promotion. The new Queen's power takes effect immediately.

37 1 N—N5 mate. Any other check permits Black to retreat his King to KB2.

38 1 Q—R6 mate. White has sacrificed both his Rooks to achieve this position.

39 1 R—R1 mate. Don't argue with necessity!

40 1 Q—B7 mate. The Black King is wedged in by his own pieces.

41 1 Q—K6 mate. The disadvantages of an exposed King in the center are obvious.

42 1 N x P mate. White has just enough pieces for this mating attack.

43 1 R—KN6 dbl. check-mate. The Black King is exposed to a discovered attack by the Bishop (on QN2) as well as the Rook. Any other 1st move by White permits Black to defend himself. Study this carefully.

44 1 N—Q5 mate.

45 1 P—N5 mate. The Pawn can kill!

46 1 R—K8 mate. Black is not defended on his 1st rank.

47 1 Q—N7 mate. This is the culmination of an attack against Black's castled King. Notice how the KN file has been ripped open.

48 1 ... B—R5 mate.

49 1 ... R—K8 mate. White cannot interpose with 2 R—B1 because this Rook is pinned by Black's Bishop.

50 1 ... N—B7 mate. This illustrates the power of the Knights.

51 1 ... N—Q6 mate. White's KP cannot capture the upstart because it is pinned: it cannot take anything because then White's King would be exposed to capture from Black's Queen.

52 1 ... Q—R5 mate. This is Black's only effective check, but it is lethal.

53 1 ... N(K5)—B7 mate. This deserves careful study, because it illustrates a double pin. 2 QxN is impossible because this would expose the King to capture from Black's Queen (on QN2). 2 RxN is also illegal because this would expose the King to capture from Black's Rook (on K8).

54 1 R—N1, K—R1 (forced); 2 B x P mate. If you solved this, it proves that you are visualizing pieces in relationship to each other and planning ahead.

55 1 Q—N8+!!, R x Q (Black must accept the Queen sacrifice); 2 N—B7 mate. Black has been forced to smother himself, and the Rook has been lured away from its defensive post.

56 1 ... R—K8+!!, 2 Q x R (if 2 N x R, Q—R8 mate; or on 2 Q—B1, Q x N mate), Q x N mate. Black's first move deflects White's pieces from their defensive posts.

57 1 ... Q x B+!!; 2 R x Q, N x RP mate. Black's timing must be accurate. No other order of moves can force mate in 2.

LESSON 6
THE ENDGAME

Endings Without Pawns on the Board

The endgame often is reached at the deliberate wish of a player who has swapped pieces in order to simplify and realize his plus. Many games do not go this far, yet it is important for you to recognize certain basic-basic positions.

The endgame is the most scientific part of chess. Most players are weak at this phase because they lack practice; they fail to win a won game or hold a drawn one because of last-minute slips — and these "slips" are all too frequent. The fact that few pieces remain on the board tends to lull one into a deceptive complacency.

WITHOUT PAWNS ON THE BOARD, IN ORDER TO MATE A LONE KING, A MATERIAL SUPERIORITY IS NEEDED OF AT LEAST FIVE UNITS ACCORDING TO THE TABLE OF RELATIVE VALUES. To put it more plainly: in order to win, one must be ahead a Rook, two Bishops, Bishop *and* Knight, or a Queen. (An important exception is two Knights. Although they total six units, it is impossible to force mate against best defense.)

Endings where both sides are even in material generally result in draws, with best play. But right now it is important to master the following elementary exercises. They are matters of technique. No amount of guesswork or trial-and-error will do.

It is important to remember that *a lone King cannot be mated in the middle of the board.* The theme of these basic positions is to drive the King to the edges of the board by fencing him in and gradually restricting his moves. This is illustrated splendidly in the case of King and Queen vs. King — a cat-and-mouse game.

King and Queen vs. King

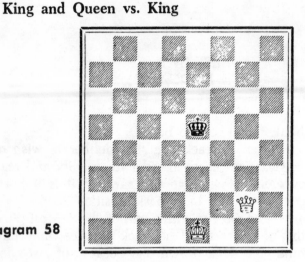

Diagram 58

White to play and win.

Ordinarily it should take only a handful of moves to win this ending. Remember the 50-move rule. If Black counts to 50 moves before White can succeed in mating him, then the game is declared drawn. If White makes a slip, it is also possible for Black to draw by stalemate.

White	Black
1 Q—B6	....

This move immediately restricts Black's choice of replies.

1	K—Q5
2 K—Q2	....

The King must cooperate to hem in Black.

2	K—K4
3 K—K3	....

Now Black is prevented from returning to Q5. Naturally Black wants to keep his King in the center as long as possible, but White relentlessly will force him to one of the corners.

3	K—B4
4 Q—Q6	....

Once more White closes in. Now Black cannot return to K4.
Slowly but surely his back is forced to the wall.

4	K—N4
5 Q—K6	K—R5
6 Q—KN6	K—R6
7 K—B3	K—R7

If instead 7 ... K—R5; then comes 8 Q—N4 mate. Black is
completely helpless.

8   Q—N2 mate

Notice the dispatch and confidence with which White closes
in for the kill. This is the trademark of the skillful player. Practice this ending until you have mastered it to your satisfaction.
Do not proceed any further until you are certain that you
could defeat even the World Champion if you had this position
against him!

King and Rook vs. King

This is slightly more difficult, but White uses the same crowd-
ing tactics. He fences Black in with his Rook and advances his
King to administer the *coup de grace*. The whole winning process should take no more than 15 moves.

Diagram 59

White to play and win.

	White	Black
1	R—R7	K—B1
2	K—K2	....

The King enters the fray.

2	....	K—N1
3	R—R7	K—B1
4	K—K3	K—K1
5	K—K4	K—Q1
6	K—Q5	K—K1
7	K—Q6	K—B1
8	K—K6	K—N1
9	K—B6	K—R1
10	K—N6!	K—N1
11	R—R8 mate	

Diagram 60

White mates in two moves.

King and Two Bishops vs. King

Diagram 61

White to play and win.

It is fairly easy to imprison the Black King by putting the Bishops alongside of each other. Bishops rake the open board via diagonals.

	White	Black
1	B—KR3	K—Q1
2	B—B4	K—K2
3	K—K2	K—B3
4	K—B3	K—K2
5	B—B5	K—B3
6	K—N4	K—K2
7	K—N5	K—Q1
8	K—B6	K—K1
9	B—B7	K—B1
10	B—Q7	K—N1
11	K—N6	K—B1
12	B—Q6ch	K—N1
13	B—K6ch	K—R1
14	B—K5 mate	

King, Bishop and Knight vs. King

Bishop and Knight vs. King is the most difficult of the elementary mates; even experienced players often fail to win it over the board. The King must be driven into a corner of the same color as the Bishop. The winning process consists of two parts: (1) driving the opposing King to the side of the board, and (2) forcing him into the right corner. Don't try to memorize the procedure, just refer to it when necessary.

Diagram 62

White to play and win.

White	Black

Again, White has 50 moves to complete his chore.

	White	Black
1	N—N3	K—Q3
2	K—N5	K—Q4
3	B—B7ch	K—K4
4	K—B5	K—B3

Black fights bravely to keep his King in the center.

	White	Black
5	B—B4	K—K4
6	N—Q2	K—B5
7	K—Q6	K—B4
8	B—Q3ch	K—B3
9	N—B3	K—B2
10	K—K5	K—N2
11	N—N5	K—N1
12	K—B6	K—B1
13	N—B7	K—N1

Now we have the basic situation where the problem is to chase the King into the other corner.

Diagram 63

White moves.

	White	Black
14	B—B5	K—B1
15	B—R7!	....

Cutting off a square and forcing the King to the left.

15	....	K—K1
16	N—K5	K—Q1
17	K—K6	K—B2
18	N—Q7	K—N2
19	B—Q3	K—B3
20	B—R6	K—B2
21	B—N5	K—Q1
22	N—N6	K—B2
23	N—Q5ch	K—Q1
24	K—Q6	K—B1
25	K—K7	K—N2
26	K—Q7	K—N1
27	B—R6	K—R2
28	B—B8	K—N1
29	N—K7	K—R2

If 29 ... K—R1; 30 K—B7, K—R2; 31 N—B6ch, K—R1; 32 B—N7 mate.

| 30 | K—B7 | K—R1 |

White now forces checkmate in two moves. Can you see it?

Diagram 64

White mates in 2 moves.

White	Black
31 B—N7ch	....

And not 31 N—B6?? — stalemate. This often happens to in-experienced players: they let their opponents out at the last minute.

| 31   .... | K—R2 |
| 32   N—B6 (or B8) mate. | |

ENDINGS WITH PAWNS ON THE BOARD
King and Queen vs. King and Pawn

An ending which occurs frequently is a Pawn on the seventh rank, supported by its King, against a Queen and a King (which is distant). If permitted to queen, the Pawn will re-establish material equality with the consequent result of a draw. Accordingly, the stronger side must prevent this from happening at all costs. Note that the Queen *always* wins against a Pawn on the sixth rank, with no exceptions. When the Pawn is on the seventh rank the Queen wins 50% of the time, depending on which file the Pawn is located.

Diagram 65

White wins by force.

The Pawn threatens to queen, thus the Queen must force the Black King to get in front of it. White then advances toward it with his King.

White	Black
1 Q—K4ch	K—B7
2 Q—Q3!	K—K8
3 Q—K3ch	K—Q8
4 K—B4	....

White keeps repeating this process and advancing his King.

4	K—B7
5 Q—B3ch!	K—Q8
6 K—Q3	K—K8

7 Q x Pch wins the Pawn and mates in three moves.

Diagram 66

The Case of the Bishop Pawn — draw.

White	Black
1 Q—N4ch	K—R7
2 Q—B3	K—N8
3 Q—N3ch	K—R8!

The point! Black can leave his Pawn unprotected because 4 Q x P allows stalemate. But 3 ... K—B8 would be a blunder

because it would allow the approach of the White King by 4
K—K4, etc.
4   Q—B3ch   K—N8
Draw by perpetual check, since White can make no headway.

Diagram 67

The Case of the Rook Pawn — draw.
White   Black

The drawing maneuver is a bit different from Diagram 66, but
Black utilizes the stalemate motif.
1   Q—N3ch   K—R8!
and White can make no headway — draw.

The proximity of the stronger King, however, can have the
most unexpected results and help the Queen to triumph as in
Diagram 68.

Diagram 68

White wins.

White	Black
1 K—K3!	....

This "quiet" move is decisive. Black is allowed to queen!

| 1 .... | P—R8=Q |
| 2 Q—B2 mate | |

King and Pawn vs. King

The possibility of queening a Pawn is the axis on which many an ending revolves. The win of a Pawn in the opening or mid-game (all other things being equal) is considered a decisive material superiority between masters. It is for this reason that I commend to the student's attention some elementary King and Pawn endings in this chapter. Once a Pawn has queened, it obviously acquires the full power of a Queen and mates accordingly. In Diagram 69, the Pawn must prevail if White is on the move and Black's King is "outside the square."

If Black were on the move, the game would end in a draw because his King could overtake the Pawn. In the lower left-hand corner of the diagram the White King is within the square, thus he cannot lose since he can catch the Pawn at his leisure whoever is on move.

Diagram 69

White to play wins; Black to move draws.

1 P—R6, K—K4; 2 P—R7, K—B3; 3 P—R8=Q+ and White wins.

If Black moves, 1 ... K—K4 draws.

Diagram 70

White to play — draw.

In end games of this sort, where one side has the advantage of a Pawn, the stronger side wins if he can get his King *in front of the pawn.* Inadvertently pushing the Pawn allows the weaker side a draw if he can get *his* King *in front of the Pawn.* Both sides, then, must race to get in front of the Pawn. If the weaker side succeeds, the game is drawn; if not, he loses.

White	Black
1 P—B5	K—B2
2 K—N5	K—N2

To abandon terrain with any other move is disastrous, e.g., 2 ... K—B1?; 3 K—B6 and White gets in front of his Pawn.

3 P—B6ch	K—B2
4 K—B5	K—B1!

The critical position. The Black King finds salvation in the "opposition." Other squares are fatal: 4 ... K—N1; 5 K—N6, K—B1; 6 P—B7, K—K2; 7 K—N7 and wins; or 4 ... K—K1; 5 K—K6, etc.

5 K—N6

....

If 5 K—K6, K—K1!

| 5 .... | K—N1! |

White is driven back since he does not have the opposition.

| 6 P—B7ch | .... |

6 K—R6, K—B2; or 6 K—B5, K—B2 is repetition. White, therefore, makes a final lunge with his Pawn.

| 6 .... | K—B1 |
| 7 K—B6 | Stalemate |

Diagram 71

White wins whoever moves.

If the stronger King reaches his sixth rank in front of his Pawn, he wins with or without the opposition, as in Diagram 71.

White to move:

White	Black
1 K—B6	K—B1
2 P—N6	K—N1
3 P—N7	K—R2
4 K—B7	K—R3
5 P—N8=Q and wins.	

Black to move:

White	Black
1	K—B1

Or 1 ... K—R1; 2 K—B7 with a similar continuation.

2 K—R7　　　　　　　　　　K—B2

3 P—N6ch and the Pawn queens unhindered.

An exception to the rule is found in the case of the Rook's Pawns. Here the lone King always obtains the draw if he gets to B1, as in diagram 72.

Diagram 72

Black draws.

　　White　　　　　　　　Black

1 P—R6　　　　　　　　　　K—B1

Not 1 ... K—K2; 2 K—N7 and wins; or even 1 ... K—B3; 2 K—N8 wins.

2 K—R8　　　　　　　　　　....

If 2 K—N6, K—N1 and Black gets to the saving square.

2 ....　　　　　　　　　　K—B2

3 P—R7　　　　　　　　　　....

Or 3 K—R7, K—B1 and a draw by repetition of moves.

3 ....　　　　　　　　　　K—B1 Stalemate!

LESSON 7
THE OPENING

The first dozen or so moves of each game comprise what is known as the opening. Unlike the endgame, most of the lines are closed and the chessboard is cluttered with pieces.

The purpose of the opening is NOT to launch an all out assault against the enemy King. Such premature tactics are bound to boomerang against halfway decent defense.

The purpose of the opening IS to bring your pieces into play continuously and rapidly. This is known as DEVELOPMENT. King safety is all-important. The King should head for shelter by castling early.

Refer to the starting lineup in diagram 2 and set it up on your own board. Note that the powerful Queen has not even got a legal move — it is hemmed in!

A basic rule of opening play is: MOBILIZE ALL YOUR RESERVES, DEPLOY THEM IN OR TOWARDS THE CENTER. What is the center and why is it so important?

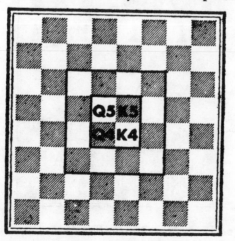

Diagram 73

PRIMARY CENTER is the inside square.
SECONDARY CENTER is the outside square.

The cluster of squares Q4, K4, Q5, K5, are the key outposts on the chessboard. In addition, there is the wider center which takes in the 12 adjacent squares. THE OPENING IS A STRUGGLE FOR CONTROL OF THE CENTER. EVERY OPENING MOVE SHOULD DEVELOP A NEW PIECE AND HAVE SOME BEARING ON THE CENTER, HOWEVER INDIRECT. PAWNS SHOULD BE PUSHED ONLY TO FREE THE PIECES WHICH ARE LOCKED BEHIND THEM.

Each player must strive to get there "fustest with the mostest." Moving the same piece twice is bad because it loses time.

Control of the center confers a space advantage. Place a Knight on K4 — notice it strikes at 8 squares. Place the same Knight at R1 — notice that it strikes at only 2 squares. A centralized piece has more mobility than a decentralized one.

Suppose White tries to take the center by storm without adequate preparation. One way of doing this might be via: 1 P—K4, P—K4; 2 P—Q4 (this is premature), P x P; 3 Q x P, N—QB3!

Diagram 73 a

Position after 3 . . . N—QB3! White's Queen is attacked (arrow) and he must lose a tempo moving it a second time. Black has wrested the initiative.

In other words, early Queen sorties are inadvisable. The Queen is a sitting duck out in the open. The minor pieces (Knights, Bishops) should be developed first — they are the advanced scouts. The major pieces (Rooks and Queens) are equivalent to the heavy artillery — it takes a long time getting them into position.

White's second move (2 P—Q4) is faulty because White must recapture with his Queen, which is uneconomical. A more logical move instead was 2 N—KB3 which (a) develops a piece and attacks Black's KP, (b) occupies a central square, (c) prepares for castling by evacuating one of the men that interferes with the connection of the King and Rook.

The middle game begins after both sides have castled and developed most of their pieces. Here is a logical sequence of moves in an opening called the *Giuoco Piano,* which is Italian for "quiet game."

SAMPLE OPENING

	White	Black
1	P—K4	P—K4
2	N—KB3	N—QB3
3	B—B4	B—B4
4	P—B3	....

Preparing for the massed advance with P-Q4. Black should continue his normal development without panic.

4	....	N—B3

Excellent! Black develops his Knight and attacks White's KP in the process.

5	P—Q4	....

This gives rise to spirited complications. Safer, but more tame, was 5 P-Q3.

4	....	P x P
5	P x P	B—N5+
6	B—Q2	....

Also playable is 6 N-B3, which involves a Pawn sacrifice after NxKP — a tricky variation for both players. (See trap #3.)

6	....	B x B+

6 ... NxKP is inferior after 7 BxB, NxB; 8 BxP+!, KxB; 9 Q-N3+, P-Q4 (best); 10 QxN, material is even but White has the better game because Black has been forced to move his King too early.

7   QNxB   ....

This also protects White's KP.

7   ....   **P—Q4!**

Otherwise White gets too strong a Pawn steamroller in the center.

8   PxP   **KNxP**
9   O—O   **O—O**
10 Q—N3   **QN—K2**
11 QR—K1   ....

White naturally seizes the open K-file with his QR, which is doing nothing.

11 ....   **P—QB3**

The chances are equal. Black has a solid game and maintains a stout blockade on his Q4 square.

Diagram 74

Position after 11 ... P—QB3. The opening is over. The real fight is now about to begin. Neither side has any marked advantage.

The battle lines are drawn in the middle game and the game begins to take on its real character.

NEVER MAKE A MOVE WITHOUT CONSIDERING YOUR OPPONENT'S REPLIES. EVERY TIME YOUR OPPONENT MAKES A MOVE, ASK YOURSELF "WHAT DOES HE THREATEN?" Here are a few principles for you to follow, especially in the opening. Like all generalizations, they should be heeded with care.

GENERAL PRINCIPLES
with Reservations

1. Avoid giving useless checks.

2. Try to prevent your opponent from castling, if possible. Castle early in the game. It puts your King in safety and brings a Rook into play.

3. Bring your Rooks into play as early as possible and place them on open files. (A file is said to be open when it is unobstructed.)

4. Do not block your Bishops by moving the King's Pawn or the Queen's Pawn one square before these pieces have been developed.

5. Develop Knights before Bishops. The course of the game determines the best square for Bishops. Knights should be developed on QB3 and KB3.

6. Doubled Pawns are undesirable as a general rule.

7. Always develop your pieces where they will have the greatest scope, mobility, and freedom of movement. Avoid cramped positions.

8. Try, even in the opening, to find moves that contain a threat.

9. Occupy, attack, or watch the center. The sides and corners are lifeless; the center radiates warmth and energy.

10. Assume that your opponent will find the right reply; do not play for traps except as a last-trench measure. (Bear in mind that frequently "the threat is stronger than the execution.")

Do not always strive to be brilliant, do not scorn simplicity.

There is simplicity in the highest flights of all art. Why not in chess?

Be wary of the "obvious" move. Each position, no matter how simple it appears, demands close study. Never play by rote.

These principles should serve as a short cut to narrow down the varied choice of moves in a given opening. Their purpose is to save time, to help you select the best move.

THE FIRST MOVE

In the original position none of the major pieces except the Knights can move. In order to get the pieces out, therefore, one of the eight Pawns should be moved. Which Pawn? The secret is to make a move that frees the greatest number of pieces, and a glance at the chessboard in the original line-up tells us that the moves 1 P–K4 and 1 P–Q4 free two pieces: the Queen and a Bishop. All other Pawn moves free only one! Logically, then, one of these two moves is best. The final choice of one or the other depends on the temperament of the player: 1 P–K4 accelerates the development of the King-side pieces to bring about castling, which is technically more rapid of execution on the King wing, as only two pieces have to move (Knight and Bishop) instead of three on the Queen side. 1 P–Q4 can be considered more solid because at Q4 the Pawn is already protected by the Queen, whereas at K4 the Pawn is entirely unprotected, which may become a cause of trouble. The hypermoderns such as Breyer even went so far as to give 1 P–K4 a question mark! Reti maintained that both of these opening moves are weak, and he proceeded to open with 1 N–KB3!

The sacrifice of a Pawn in the opening to obtain development and secure territory is fairly frequent. These *gambits* used to delight our ancestors but are less highly appreciated in our scientific age, where the resulting threats and compensations have been thoroughly investigated.

The following series of columns are to be read straight down the page. White's move is above the line, Black's below. **Key:** =Equal position; $\pm$ White stands better; $\mp$ Black stands better.

KING PAWN OPENINGS

1	P–K4 / P–K4	P–K4 / P–K4	P–K4 / P–K4	P–K4 / P–K3	P–K4 / P–K3	P–K4 / P–QB3
2	N–KB3 / N–QB3	P–KB4 / P x P	N–KB3 / N–KB3	P–Q4 / P–Q4	P–Q4 / P–Q4	P–Q4 / P–Q4
3	B–N5	N–KB3 / P–Q4	N x P / P–Q3 (a)	N–QB3 / B–N5	N–QB3 / N–KB3	N–QB3 / P x P
4	The Ruy Lopez	P x P / N–KB3	N–KB3 / N x P	P–K5 / P–QB4	P–K5 / KN–Q2	N x P / B–B4
5		King's Gambit Accepted	Q–K2 / Q–K2	P–QR3 / B x Nch	QN–K2 / P–QB4	N–N3 / B–N3
6			P–Q3 / N–KB3	P x B =	P–QB3 / N–QB3	P–KR4 / P–KR4
7			B–N5 / Q x Qch	French Defense	P–KB4 / Q–N3	N–B3 / N–Q2
8			B x Q / B–K2		N–B3 / P–B3	B–Q3 / B x B
9			N–B3 / B–Q2		P–QR3 / P x KP	Q x B / KN–B3
10			O–O / O–O =		BP x P / P x P	B–Q2 ±
11			Petroff Defense		P x P ± / French Defense	Caro-Kann Defense

(a) Not 3 ... N x P?; 4 Q–K2, N–KB3; 5 N–B6 dis ch winning the Queen; or if 4 . . . P–Q4; 5 P–Q3 and White wins a piece. See diagram 75.

THE RUY LOPEZ

1 P–K4, P–K4; 2 N–KB3, N–QB3; 3 B–N5, P–QR3 (Morphy's Defense).

4 B–R4 (b)	B–R4	B–R4	B–R4	B–R4	B x N (i)
N–B3	N–B3	N–B3	N–B3	P–Q3 (h)	QP x B
5 O–O	O–O	O–O	O–O	P–B3	P–Q4 (j)
N x P (c)	B–K2 (d)	B–K2	B–K2	B–Q2	P x P
6 P–Q4	R–K1	R–K1	Q–K2 (f)	P–Q4	Q x P
P–QN4	P–QN4	P–QN4	P–QN4	N–B3	Q x Q
7 B–N3	B–N3	B–N3	B–N3	O–O	N x Q
P–Q4	P–Q3	O–O	P–Q3	B–K2	B–Q2
8 P x P	P–B3	P–B3	P–QR4	P–Q5	N–QB3
B–K3	N–QR4	P–Q4!?(e)	R–QN1	N–QN1	O–O–O
9 P–B3	B–B2	P x P	P x P	B–B2	B–K3
B–K2	P–B4	N x P	P x P	B–N5	P–KN3
10 QN–Q2	P–Q4	N x P	P–B3	P–B4	O–O–O
O–O	Q–B2	N x N	B–N5	QN–Q2	P–KR3=
11 Q–K2	P–KR3	R x N	R–Q1	P–KR3	
N–B4	O–O	P–QB3	O–O	B–R4	
12 N–Q4	QN–Q2	P–Q4	P–Q4	N–B3	
N x B!	BP x P	B–Q3	P x P (g)	O–O	
13 QN x N	P x P	R–K1	P x P	P–KN4	
Q–Q2	N–B3	Q–R5	P–Q4	B–N3	
14 N x N	P–Q5	P–N3	P–K5	Q–K2	
Q x N	N–QN5	Q–R6	N–K5	N–K1	
15 B–K3	B–N1	Q–B3 ±	N–B3 ±	B–Q2 ∓	
B–KB4=	P–QR4=				

(b) This retains the pressure. If 4 B x N, QP x B; 5 N x P, Q–Q5 advantageously regains the Pawn. White's aim is to develop quickly.

(c) The Open Defense.

(d) The Closed Defense.

(e) Marshall's Attack. Black sacrifices a Pawn for the initiative.

(f) The Worrall Attack.

(g) White was threatening to win a piece with 13 P–Q5.

(h) The Steinitz Defense Deferred.

(i) The Exchange Variation. White gives up the "two Bishops" in order to double Black's Pawns; his advantage is in the end game.

(j) Again if 5 N x P, Q–Q5! (See note b.)

"Although very satisfactory weapons have been found lately to prove full equality for Black, the Ruy Lopez comes nearer than any other opening to conferring a lasting advantage with the move. White controls the center, his pieces have greater mobility than those of his adversary, and the opening often may yield him an immediate and enduring attack"—*Modern Chess Openings*.

When Black does not wish to relinquish the initiative, he chooses other replies to 1 P–K4 than 1 ... P–K4. These used to be called "irregular," but they have become so standardized that they have all been given names. The most fighting defense at Black's disposal is the Sicilian.

SICILIAN DEFENSE   1 P–K4, P–QB4

#					
2	N–KB3	N–KB3	N–KB3	N–KB3	N–QB3
	P–Q3	P–Q3	N–QB3	P–Q3	N–QB3
3	P–Q4	P–QN4!? (c)	P–Q4	P–Q4	KN–K2
	P x P	P x P (d)	P x P	P x P	P–KN3
4	N x P	P–Q4	N x P	N x P	P–KN3
	N–KB3	N–KB3	N–B3	N–KB3	B–N2
5	N–QB3 (a)	B–Q3	N–QB3	N–QB3	B–N2
	P–KN3	P–Q4	P–K3 (e)	P–QR3	P–K3!
6	B–K2	QN–Q2	B–K3	P–KN3	P–Q3
	B–N2	P x P	P–Q3	P–K4 (f)	KN–K2
7	B–K3	N x P	B–K2	N(4)–K2	O–O
	O–O	QN–Q2	B–K2	B–K3	O–O
8	O–O	N(K4)–N5	O–O	B–N2	B–K3
	N–B3	Q–B2	O–O	QN–Q2	P–N3
9	N–N3 (b)	P–QB4!	N–N3	O–O	Q–Q2
	B–K3	P–KR3	P–QR3	P–QN4	P–Q4
10	P–B4	N–R3	P–B4∓	P–B4	P x P
	N–QR4=	P–KN4∓		R–B1=(g)	P x P=

(a) The Dragon Variation.

(b) To prevent 9 ... P—Q4 which would free Black's position.

(c) The Wing Gambit Deferred, championed by Paul Keres.

(d) Black can advantageously decline by 3 ... N—KB3; 4 P x P, N x P=.

(e) The Scheveningen Variation.

(f) The Modern Variation.

(g) From the game Seidman-Evans, United States Championship, 1951.

In every opening Black is said to do well if he can achieve "equality." The term does not, contrary to popular belief, mean that a draw should result with best play by both sides; it does, however, indicate that both sides have an "approximately" equal chance to win: the better player will win either side of the position.

QUEEN PAWN OPENINGS

In modern master play it is customary to open the game with 1 P—Q4. The move has the effect of postponing tactical play until late in the middle game when both players have developed their pieces. On the whole, the Queen's Pawn openings lead to more subtle and refined positional jockeying than the King's Pawn.

QUEEN'S GAMBIT

1	P–Q4	P–Q4	P–Q4	P–Q4	P–Q4
	P–Q4	P–Q4	N–KB3	N–KB3	N–KB3
2	P–QB4	P–QB4	P–QB4	P–QB4	P–QB4
	P x P	P–K3 (a)	P–K3	P–K3	P–KN3
3	N–KB3	N–QB3	N–QB3	N–KB3	N–QB3
	N–KB3	N–KB3	B–N5	P–QN3	P–Q4
4	P–K3	B–N5	P–K3	P–KN3	P x P
	P–K3	QN–Q2	O–O	B–N2	N x P
5	B x P	P–K3	N–K2	B–N2	P–K4
	P–B4	B–K2	P–Q4	B–K2	N x N
6	O–O	N–B3	P–QR3	O–O	P x N
	P–QR3	O–O	B–K2	O–O	P–QB4
7	Q–K2	R–B1	P x P	N–B3	B–QB4
	N–B3	P–B3	N x P	N–K5	B–N2
8	R–Q1	B–Q3	Q–B2!	Q–B2	N–K2
	P–QN4	P x P	N–KB3	N x N	O–O
9	B–N3	B x P	P–KN3	Q x N	O–O
	Q–N3	N–Q4!	P–B4	P–KB4	P x P
10	P–QR4	B x B ±	B–N2 ± (b)	N–K1± (c)	P x P ±
	B–N2 =				

Queen's Gambit Accepted	Queen's Gambit Declined	Nimzo-Indian Defense	Queen's Indian Defense	Gruenfeld Defense

(a) The Orthodox Defense.

(c) Euwe-Evans, Wertheim Memorial Tournament, New York, 1951.

(b) Evans-Reshevsky, United States Championship, New York, 1951.

When I first started to play I thought that the Queen's Gambit meant the sacrifice of a Queen — far from it! It has been truly said that when White plays 1 P–Q4 he should play to force P–K4 advantageously at some future point. Accordingly, White undermines Black's Pawn on Q4 by playing 2 P–QB4.

The "gambit" refers to the temporary sacrifice of a Pawn; by trying to hold it, Black gets much the worst of the position.

TEN TRICKS AND TRAPS

No. 1 RUY LOPEZ — NOAH'S ARK TRAP
1 P—K4, P—K4; 2 N—KB3, N—QB3; 3 B—N5, P—QR3; 4 B —R4, N—B3; 5 N—B3, P—Q3; 6 P—Q4, P—QN4; 7 B—N3, P x P; 8 N x P? (White can still save himself with 8 B—Q5), N x N; 9 Q x N, P—B4; 10 Q—any, P—B5 and wins a Bishop.

No. 2 RUY LOPEZ—CLOSED VARIATION
1 P—K4, P—K4; 2 N—KB3, N—QB3; 3 B—N5, P—QR3; 4 B—R4, N—B3; 5 O—O, B—K2; 6 R—K1, P—QN4; 7 B—N3, P—Q3; 8 P—B3, N—QR4; 9 B—B2, P—B4; 10 P—Q4, Q—B2; 11 P—QR4, QR—N1; 12 RP x P, RP x P; 13 P x KP, P x P; 14 N x P? (So far so good, but now White plays to win a Pawn based on the fact that Black's Queen is overburdened; 14 QN—Q2 is correct), Q x N; 15 R x N, N—N5; 16 P—B4 (16 P—KN3 fails against . . . Q—R4; 17 P—R4, P—N4 with a winning attack), Q—B2; 17 R—R1, P—B5!; 18 R—K2, Q—N3ch; 19 K—B1, N x Pch; 20 K—K1, Q—N8ch; 21 K—Q2, N—B8ch; 22 K—K1, N—K6ch and wins the Queen.

No. 3 GIUOCO PIANO
1 P—K4, P—K4; 2 N—KB3, N—QB3; 3 B—B4, B—B4; 4 P—B3, N—B3; 5 P—Q4, P x P; 6 P x P, B—N5ch; 7 N—B3, N x KP; 8 O—O, B x N; 9 P—Q5, N—K4!; 10 P x B, N x B; 11 Q—Q4, N(B5)—Q3? (holding the piece is fatal; Black gets a satisfactory position after 11 . . . P—KB4!; 12 Q x N, P—Q3); 12 Q x NP, Q—B3; 13 Q x Q, N x Q; 14 R—K1ch, K—B1 (if 14 . . . K—Q1; 15 B—N5); 15 B—R6ch, K—N1; 16 R—K5 N(B3)—K5; 17 R—K1, P—KB4; 18 R—K7, P—N3; 19 N—R4!, B—N2; 20 P—B3, N—B2; 21 N x P, N(K5)—Q3; 22 R—K8ch!, R x R; 23 R x Rch, N x R; 24 N—K7 mate.

No. 4 EVANS GAMBIT DECLINED

1 P—K4, P—K4; 2 N—KB3, N—QB3; 3 B—B4, B—B4; 4 P—QN4, B—N3; 5 P—N5, N—Q5; 6 N x P??, Q— N4; 7 N x BP, Q x KNP; 8 R—B1, Q x KPch; 9 B—K2, N—B6 mate. (See diagram 79.)

No. 5 PHILIDOR'S DEFENSE

1 P—K4, P—K4; 2 N—KB3, P—Q3; 3 B—B4, P—KR3; 4 N—B3, B—N5? (4 . . . N—KB3 is essential); 5 N x KP!, B x Q? (relatively better is 5 . . . P x N; 6 Q x B, though White should still win easily with his material advantage of a Pawn); 6 B x Pch, K—K2; 7 N—Q5 mate. (See diagram 44.)

No. 6 PHILIDOR'S DEFENSE

1 P—K4, P—K4; 2 N—KB3, P—Q3; 3 P—Q4, N—Q2; 4 B—QB4, P—QB3; 5 N—N5, N—R3; 6 P—QR4, B—K2? (that this plausible move should lose is a tribute to the subtlety of the trap; correct is 6 . . . N—N3∓); 7 B x Pch!, N x B; 8 N—K6, Q—N3 (or 8 . . . Q—R4ch; 9 B—Q2, Q—N3; 10 P—R5, Q x NP; 11 B—B3, Q—N4; 12 N—B7ch winning the Queen); 9 P—R5, Q—N5ch; 10 B—Q2, Q—B5 (if 10 . . . Q x NP; 11 B—B3 wins the Queen); 11 N—B7 ch, K—Q1; 12 P—QN3, Q x QP; 13 N—K6ch wins the Queen. (See diagram 78.)

No. 7 FRENCH DEFENSE

1 P—K4, P—K3; 2 P—Q4, P—Q4; 3 N—QB3, P x P; 4 N x P, N—Q2; 5 N—KB3, KN—B3; 6 N x Nch, N x N; 7 B—Q3, B—K2; 8 Q—K2, O—O; 9 B—KN5, P—QN3??; 10 B x N, B x B; 11 Q—K4 wins a Rook because of the double threat of 12 Q x P mate and 12 Q x R. (See diagram 77.)

No. 8 CARO-KANN DEFENSE

A grandmaster was once mated in eleven moves! Here is the game, played in Vienna, in 1910, between Richard Reti (White) and Savielly Tartakower (Black): 1 P—K4, P—QB3; 2 P—Q4, P—Q4; 3 N—QB3, P x P; 4 N x P, N—B3; 5 Q—3,

P—K4!? (risky; better is 5...QN—Q2); **6 P x P, Q—R4ch; 7 B—Q2, Q x KP; 8 O—O—O!, N x N?; 9 Q—Q8ch!!, K x Q; 10 B—N5 dis ch, K—B2** (or 10...K—K1; 11 R—Q8 mate); **11 B—Q8 mate.** (See diagram 76.)

No. 9 DANISH GAMBIT

1 P—K4, P—K4; 2 P—Q4, P x P; 3 P—QB3, P x P; 4 B—QB4, P x P; 5 B x P, P—Q4!; 6 B x QP, N—KB3; 7 N—QB3 (if 7 B x Pch, K x B; 8 Q x Q, B—N5 ch; 9 Q—Q2, B x Qch ∓), **N B; 8 N x N, P—QB3?** (8...N—B3 is correct); **9 N—B6ch!, P x N; 10 Q x Qch, K x Q; 11 B x Pch, K—K1; 12 B x R** and wins the exchange.

No. 10 QUEEN'S GAMBIT — EXCHANGE VARIATION

Here is a trap into which the immortal Akiba Rubinstein fell twice! If he could, you can too. **1 P—Q4, P—Q4; 2 P—QB4, P—K3; 3 N—QB3, N—KB3; 4 B—N5, QN—Q2; 5 P—K3, B—K2; 6 N—B3, O—O; 7 R—B1, P—B3; 8 Q—B2, P—QR3; 9 P x P, KP x P; 10 B—Q3, R—K1; 11 O—O, P—R3; 12 B—KB4, N—R4?** (correct is 12...P—B4); **13 N x P!, P x N?** (Rubinstein resigned himself to the loss of a Pawn by 13 N x B); **14 B—B7** winning the Queen. (See diagram 80.)

LESSON 8
WINNING TACTICS

Your opponent has no intention of handing you the game on a silver platter, or of leaving his pieces up for grab. It is always good to adopt a policy of "watchful waiting," but this may yield no results. It is important to recognize certain tactical themes when they occur. To develop a quick eye you must spot potential weaknesses in the enemy camp. No angel is perched on your shoulder to signal the presence of a combination. Follow these simple steps to size up any position at a glance:
1. Is material even? If not, who is ahead?
2. Who is on move? Is anything attacked? Are there any threats?
3. Who is better developed? Who controls the center and open lines? Are any men still on their home bases?

4. Who has the better Pawn Structure? Has one side made too many Pawn moves and neglected development?
Position play is the art of consolidating your game in small ways when no direct combination is possible. You should not expect to win unless you have first built up some advantage in material, time, or space. The player who tries to force the issue should not be able to succeed against best defense.

A chess brilliancy is similar to a home run in baseball. Sometimes it comes like a bolt from the blue! Here are several frequent tactical motifs. Once familiar with them, you too can be brilliant.

DISCOVERED ATTACK. This is particularly vicious when it takes the form of a check: one piece moves, unmasking the action of a man behind it. Diagram 75 is an illustration of a stinging discovered check. ("Discovered" is used in the sense of "uncovered.") It arises from a trap in Petroff's Defense: 1 P—K4, P—K4; 2 N—KB3, N—KB3; 3 N x P, N x P?; 4 Q—K2!, N—KB3?; 5 N—B6 dis. ch!, winning Black's Queen.

Diagram 75

If White moves his Knight to the square indicated by the arrow, he will unmask a check to Black's King (from his Queen). Whatever Black does to block the check, White takes the Queen with his Knight.

This discovered check is very dangerous to the defender because of the possibility of a double attack. The check *must* be met. How? One way is with **5 . . . B—K2.** Then what would White do? Simply **6 N x Q.** Winning an opponent's Queen is almost as satisfying as checkmating him!

DOUBLE CHECK. This merely means that the King is attacked from 2 different directions at the same time. This is nastier than a discovered check. Diagram 76 from trap #8 in our last lesson.

White sacrificed his Queen to maneuver the Black King into this unhealthy position. Black has two squares to move his King and sudden death follows either way. If **1 . . . K—K1;** White comes down with his Rook and says checkmate — **2 R—Q8!** If **1 . . . K—B1;** White slides in with his Bishop with checkmate — **2 B—Q8!**

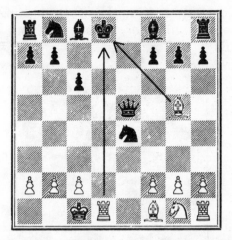

Diagram 76

Black's King is attacked by the Bishop AND Rook (see arrows). The King must move — where can it go?

FORKING ATTACKS. This is a simultaneous double threat against two *different* enemy units. (The double check is focused only against the enemy King.) Diagram 77 arises from trap #7 in the French Defense. Diagram 78 depicts trap #6 in Philidor's Defense. In both cases, Black is helpless against forking attacks.

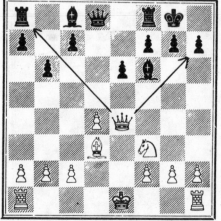

Diagram 77

A Queen fork. The double threat of Q x P mate OR Q x R (see arrows) gains White a Rook.

Black must defend his King. How? By playing **1 ... P—N3.** Then what would White do? Simply carry out his secondary threat: **2 Q x R.**

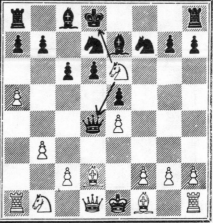

Diagram 78

A Knight fork. Black must move his King out of check, whereupon White's Knight snatches the hapless Queen — see arrows.

PINNING ATTACKS. The pin is mightier than the sword! To pin a piece is to paralyze its movement: if it moves, it exposes an even more valuable piece behind it to capture. Diagram 79 comes from trap #4. Diagram 80 illustrates trap #10.

Diagram 79

White is checkmated (see arrow). The Bishop cannot capture the checking Knight because it is pinned to the King.

White's Bishop on K2 is subject to an absolute pin: it is illegal for it to move – why? Because it would expose the King to capture from Black's Queen.

Diagram 80

A subtle pin. Black's Pawn is free to capture the Knight (arrow), but this would be unwise. Why?

DEFLECTING MANEUVERS. Ever have your hands full when someone asked you for a match? Blow a fuse by overloading an electric socket? A chess piece, occupied with too many chores, is equally vulnerable. When a man is burdened with a defensive task, it may be possible to induce a nervous breakdown by piling on one more straw.

Thus 1 R—Q8+!, K x R (forced); 2 Q x Q, R—B1; 3 N—K5 (or Q x RP) leads to a quick win. White emerges with an overwhelming material advantage. In chess, as in advertising, it sometimes pays to give a little in order to get a lot!

Here is still another example of ruthless logic, this time culminating in checkmate. Visualization is the ability to picture the position in your mind without actually moving the pieces – see how that comes in handy here! The theme is smothered mate.

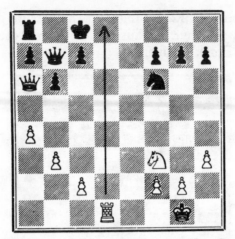

Diagram 81

Black's King has the task of protecting the Queen. White (on move) gains nothing merely by swapping Queens. But he can deflect the King with a temporary Rook sacrifice (arrow). The King must take the Rook to get out of check, but this leaves the Queen unguarded.

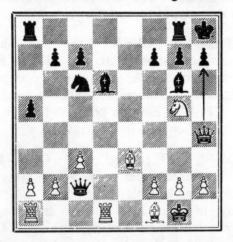

Diagram 82

Black's King apparently is well guarded. White (on move) shatters this illusion by a startling Queen sacrifice (arrow). After 1 Q x P+!!, B x Q; 2 N x P mate.

In other words, White sacrificed his Queen in order to deflect Black's Bishop (on KN3) from defense of the KBP. In the final position all Black's escape squares for the King are smothered by his own pieces!

X-RAY ATTACKS. An X-ray is similar to a pin, except that the more valuable unit is first in the line of fire — when it moves away, it exposes a unit behind it to capture. Diagram 83 illustrates the deadly simplicity of this theme.

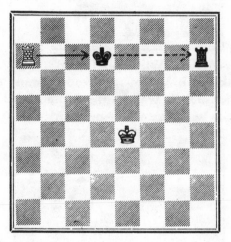

Diagram 83

A lethal X-ray check! Black's King must move, but the Rook (behind it) is doomed.

1 ... K—any; 2 R x R transposes into the elementary win analyzed in diagrams 59 and 60.

Here are 20 exercises designed to test your powers of recognition. Each problem employs a theme already discussed. The solutions follow diagram 103.

4 DEFLECTING MANEUVERS

Diagram 84

BLACK MOVES AND WINS MATERIAL
White's Rook (on B1) is overworked. It must defend the other Rook (on B3) as well as the Bishop (on Q1). But no man can serve two masters — prove it!

Diagram 85

WHITE MOVES AND WINS MATERIAL
This is the essence of chess logic: when A defends B, undermine A. Black's Rook is needed to guard the Queen. How can White force Black to remove this guard?

Diagram 86

WHITE TO PLAY AND WIN
Black's Queen and Rook are both tied down to prevent
the invasion of White's Queen. One strong gust of wind
destroys this delicate defensive setup.
(Hint: Keep your eye on the open QR file.)

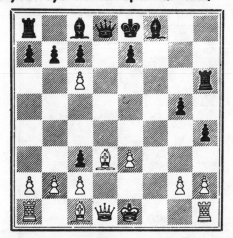

Diagram 87

WHITE MATES IN 2 MOVES
Black's K-Rook is overburdened: it must guard against
both B—N6 and/or Q—R5. With an electrifying first move,
White assures himself a successful invasion.
(Hint: Look for a Queen sacrifice and a follow-up.)

4 DISCOVERED ATTACK EXERCISES

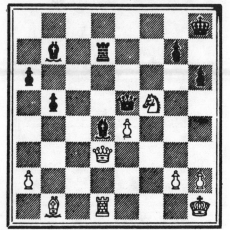

Diagram 88

BLACK MOVES AND WINS MATERIAL
Remember, a discovered attack is set up by the removal of a piece. When this game was played, in 1902, Black resigned — thinking his Bishop (on Q5) was doomed because of the pin. But there is a ray of sunshine — find it!

Diagram 89

WHITE MOVES AND WINS THE QUEEN
Black's undefended Queen forms the basis of a nasty discovered attack. (Hint: If Black's King were on KR1, he would have a sound position.)

Diagram 90

WHITE MOVES. WHY CAN'T HIS QUEEN TAKE THE UN-
DEFENDED KNIGHT (ON Q4)?
(Hint: It would cost too much.)

Diagram 91

WHITE MATES IN 1 MOVE
Here is a discovered double checkmate — a real stinger!

4 FORKING EXERCISES

Diagram 92

WHITE MOVES AND WINS A PAWN

Here is a 4 move combination in which White manages to win a Pawn, clear all the pieces off the board, and emerge with a decisive advantage in the King and Pawn endgame.

Diagram 93

WHITE MOVES AND WINS MATERIAL

Material is even, but Black is behind in development —— his Q-Bishop is still hemmed in. White can create a double threat resulting in the win of a piece. (Hint: Black's B on K2 is a danger spot.)

Diagram 94

WHITE MOVES AND WINS MATERIAL
Black's 2 developed men (the Bishop and Knight) are
scattered ineffectively. Both are unprotected. A potent
Queen fork brings home the bacon.
(Hint: What move can White make which attacks 2 enemy
pieces simultaneously?)

Diagram 95

BLACK MOVES AND WINS MATERIAL
White is a Pawn ahead, but his pieces are posted de-
fensively and his Bishop has no scope.
(Hint: The Bishop is the hero of this fork.)

4 PINNING EXERCISES

Diagram 96

WHITE MOVES AND WINS MATERIAL
White can initiate the pin. He has a golden opportunity to win Black's Queen.

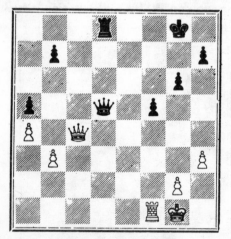

Diagram 97

WHITE MOVES AND WINS MATERIAL
White can pile up on a pinned piece, thus intensifying the pressure.
(Hint: use the X-ray attack.)

Diagram 98

BLACK MOVES AND WINS MATERIAL.
Black can create a pin. But how can he set one up, with what order of moves?

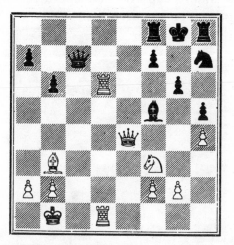

Diagram 99

WHITE MATES IN 2 MOVES
The pinner pinned! Black thinks he can win the Queen, but comes a rude shock!
(Hint: White executes an existing pin.)

4 X-RAY EXERCISES

Diagram 100

WHITE TO PLAY AND WIN
White would like to queen his Pawn, but the Rook is in
its path. This is his dilemma: if the Rook moves away,
Black's Rook simply captures the unprotected Pawn.
(Hint: Study diagram 83 carefully.)

Diagram 101

WHITE MOVES AND WINS MATERIAL
Black's Queen and Rook are dangerously aligned on the
same diagonal, and his Bishop has not yet developed on
QN2. How can White exploit this present setup?

Diagram 102

WHITE TO PLAY AND WIN
Black threatens mate on the move and is a Rook ahead to boot. Clearly, this is no time to dawdle. By a proper series of checks, White can force the win of Black's Queen. (Hint: Check, check!)

Diagram 103

BLACK MOVES AND WINS MATERIAL
White is just holding on by a hair. Black, with a forceful series of moves, can win the undefended Rook (on K6). (Hint: Check, check, check!)

SOLUTIONS

84   1 ... R x B !; 2 R x R, Q x R. Black emerges a Bishop ahead.

85   1 R—B8+!, R x R (forced); 2 Q x Q.

86   1 R x P!!, R x R (or if 1 ... Q x R; 2 Q—Q7 mate); 2 Q—Q8 mate.

87   1 Q—R5+!, R x Q; 2 B—N6 mate.

88   1 ... B—N8!!; 2 Q x R, Q x P mate. (If 2 K x B, R x Q leads to a won endgame.)

89   1 N—R6+, K—R1; 2 Q x Q.

90   If 1 Q x N?, N—N5+!; 2 P x N, B x Q. Black wins a Queen (10 units) in return for 2 Knights (6 units). White's best move is probably 1 P—B4. He should ignore the tempting bait.

91   1 N—B6 discovered double checkmate!!

92   1 Q—Q8+, K—N2; 2 Q x N+, K x Q; 3 N x P+, K—any; 4 N x Q, P x N; 5 K—B1, White is a Pawn ahead in the King and Pawn endgame. With proper technique, he should win.

93   1 Q—K4, P—KN3 (in order to defend against 2 Q x P mate); 2 Q x B. White wins the Bishop.

94   1 Q—N4. Black cannot save both his pieces with one move.

95   1 ... R x B!; 2 R x R, B x P+; 3 K — any, B x R. Black winds up a Bishop ahead.

96   1 B—N5!

97   1 R—Q1!!, Q x Q; 2 R x R+, K—B2; 3 P x Q. White is a Rook ahead.

98   1 ... Q x P+!!: 2 Q x Q, R x R!; 3 Q x B) (forced), P x B. Black ends up an exchange ahead — this, plus his extra Pawn, is enough to win.

99   1 R x P+!, B x R; 2 Q x B mate. Black's Pawn cannot take the Queen because it is pinned.

100   1 R—R8 (1 R—KN8 or KB8 will also do), R x P (Black can give a few checks first, but eventually he must capture this Pawn or White simply queens it); 2 R—R7+, K—any; 3 R x R.

101 1 B—B3!, Q—any; 2 B x R and wins. (If 1 . . . N—Q4; 2 N
x N!, P x N; 3 B x P leads to the same debacle for Black.)

102 1 Q—N7+, K—B4 (if 1 . . . K—R4; 2 Q—R7+, K—N4; 3
Q x Q wins); 2 Q—Q7+, K—any; 3 Q x Q.

103 1 . . . Q x Q+; 2 K x Q, R—Q8+; 3 K—K2, R—K8+!; 4
K—any, R x R.

LESSON 9
EXERCISES IN COMBINATION PLAY

Of all the qualities which make a chessplayer, imagination, patience, foresight, and LOGIC are predominant. Can anyone play brilliant chess, or is it a knack imparted at birth to the chosen few? Fortunately, any problem on the chessboard can be solved by the stern application of logic. Some players are more talented than others, but chess is an inexhaustible well from which even the novice may draw refreshment.

THE PRIMARY OBJECT OF COMBINATION PLAY IS TO FORCE CHECKMATE OR WIN MATERIAL. AN INITIAL SACRIFICE USUALLY STARTS THE BALL ROLLING. Any player can overlook a brilliant continuation over-the-board, especially if he does not suspect the presence of a trick in the position.

The purpose of this section is to delight you with some of the most beautiful and profound moves ever played on a chessboard. Here are 60 famous settings taken from the games of Alekhine, Lasker, Capablanca, Morphy, Botvinnik, and a host of other chess immortals. Each position contains a winning idea for the side on move. Some of the variations are quite long, but most are forced: in other words, the loser has only one move each time in order to avoid immediate catastrophe; on the other hand, the winner cannot afford to make one slip in his timing.

IN ORDER TO SOLVE THESE PROBLEMS YOU HAVE TO CALCULATE THE BEST MOVES FOR THE LOSER AS WELL AS THE WINNER. THERE IS ONLY ONE CORRECT CONTINUATION. THE FIRST MOVE IS USUALLY THE KEY.

These exercises are not easy. But here is an opportunity for you to follow in the footsteps of the world's great masters. The element of deception in chess is at a minimum because everything is open and above board, there are no "closed hands." Look for forceful, hard-hitting key moves.

The solutions follow diagram 163. Don't be ashamed to peek! Do not be discouraged if you find a good many of these problems over your head. Spend as much time as necessary on each position until you understand it thoroughly.

The mistakes are all there, waiting to be made. Go to it!

Diagram 104   **Diagram 105**

WHITE MOVES FIRST   **WHITE MOVES FIRST**

Diagram 106

Diagram 107

WHITE MOVES FIRST

WHITE MOVES FIRST

Diagram 108

Diagram 109

BLACK MOVES FIRST

BLACK MOVES FIRST

Diagram 110

BLACK MOVES FIRST

Diagram 111

BLACK MOVES FIRST

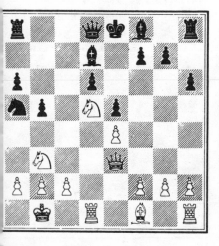

Diagram 112

WHITE MOVES FIRST

Diagram 113

WHITE MOVES FIRST

Diagram 114

WHITE MOVES FIRST

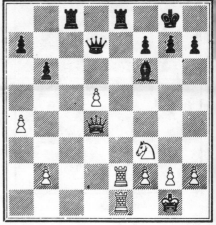

Diagram 115

WHITE MOVES FIRST

Diagram 116

BLACK MOVES FIRST

Diagram 117

BLACK MOVES FIRST

Diagram 118

Diagram 119

BLACK MOVES FIRST

BLACK MOVES FIRST

Diagram 120

Diagram 121

WHITE MOVES FIRST

WHITE MOVES FIRST

Diagram 122

Diagram 123

WHITE MOVES FIRST

WHITE MOVES FIRST

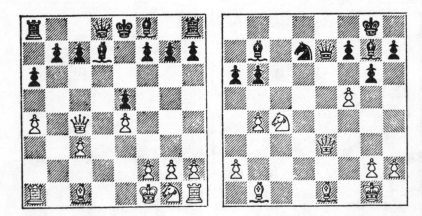

Diagram 124

Diagram 125

BLACK MOVES FIRST

BLACK MOVES FIRST

Diagram 126

BLACK MOVES FIRST

Diagram 127

BLACK MOVES FIRST

Diagram 128

WHITE MOVES FIRST

Diagram 129

WHITE MOVES FIRST

Diagram 130

WHITE MOVES FIRST

Diagram 131

WHITE MOVES FIRST

Diagram 132

BLACK MOVES FIRST

Diagram 133

BLACK MOVES FIRST

Diagram 134

BLACK MOVES FIRST

Diagram 135

BLACK MOVES FIRST

Diagram 136

WHITE MOVES FIRST

Diagram 137

WHITE MOVES FIRST

Diagram 138

Diagram 139

WHITE MOVES FIRST

WHITE MOVES FIRST

Diagram 140

Diagram 141

BLACK MOVES FIRST

BLACK MOVES FIRST

Diagram 142

BLACK MOVES FIRST

Diagram 143

BLACK MOVES FIRST

Diagram 144

WHITE MOVES FIRST

Diagram 145

WHITE MOVES FIRST

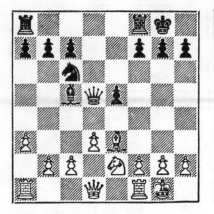

Diagram 146

WHITE MOVES FIRST

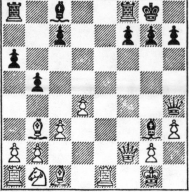

Diagram 147

WHITE MOVES FIRST

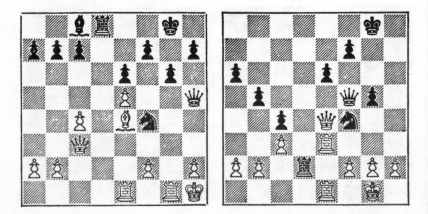

Diagram 148

BLACK MOVES FIRST

Diagram 149

BLACK MOVES FIRST

Diagram 150

BLACK MOVES FIRST

Diagram 151

BLACK MOVES FIRST

Diagram 152

WHITE MOVES FIRST

Diagram 153

WHITE MOVES FIRST

Diagram 154

WHITE MOVES FIRST

Diagram 155

WHITE MOVES FIRST

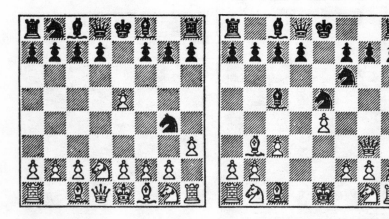

Diagram 156

BLACK MOVES FIRST

Diagram 157

BLACK MOVES FIRST

Diagram 158

BLACK MOVES FIRST

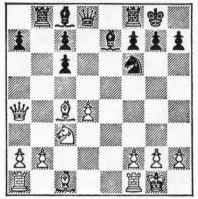

Diagram 159

BLACK MOVES FIRST

Diagram 160

WHITE MOVES FIRST

Diagram 161

WHITE MOVES FIRST

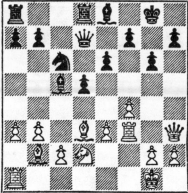

Diagram 162   **Diagram 163**

WHITE MOVES FIRST   **WHITE MOVES FIRST**

SOLUTIONS

104   White is a Pawn down and apparently has no forceful continuation. But Alekhine finds the brilliant touch: **1 R x N+!; K x R; 2 Q x R+!!, P x Q; 3 R—B8+** and mate follows.

105   White is two pieces down and his Rook is attacked. It is do-or-die! **1 Q—Q8+!!, K x Q; 2 B—N5 dbl ch, K—K1** (or 2 . . . K—B2; 3 B—Q8 mate); **3 R—Q8 mate.**

106   White rips through with **1 N x P!, P x N** (1 . . . N x N?; 2 Q x P mate); **2 Q x N!!, P x Q; 3 R—N1+, K—R1; 4 B x P mate.**

107   White's Knight seems pinned, but this is an illusion: **1 N x P!!, B x Q** (relatively better is 1 . . . PxN; 2 Q x B, but White remains a Pawn ahead in this variation); **2 B x P+, K—K2; 3 N—Q5 mate.**

108   A potent discovered check is in the air: **1 . . . Q—Q7+!!; 2 Q x Q, P—K6 dis. ch; 3 K—N1, R—R8 mate.**

109   Timing is important: **1 . . . N—K5!** (not first 1 . . . Q x Q+?; 2 K x Q, N—K5+; 3 K—K2! holds everything); **2 Q x Q**

(or 2 P x N, R x R and mate follows); **R x R mate.**

110 **1...B x P!!** threatening Q—N7 mate; **2 R x B** (if 2 N x B, Q x R+ wins material), **R—K8+; 3 K—R2, R—R8 mate.** The weakness of White's 1st rank is fatal.

111 A neat pin decides the issue: **1...R—K8!!; 2 R x R, R x R; 3 Q x R** (forced), **Q—N7 mate.**

112 Black's pieces are badly placed. White wins the exchange with **1 Q—N6!!, Q x Q** (not 1...N x N; 2 N—B7+, K—K2; 3 Q x P mate); **2 N x Q, N x N** (if 2...R—QN1; 3 N x B, K x N; 4 N x N); **3 N x R,** etc. (1 N—N6 doesn't work after N x N; 2 N x R, N—B4; 3 P—N4, N—R5.)

113 Black is 2 pieces ahead, but he succumbs to a Queen sacrifice: **1 Q x P+!!, K x Q; 2 P—R8=Q+!!** (a vital finesse; not 2 R—N5+?, K—R1 and wins), **R x Q; 3 R—N5+, K—B1; 4 R x R mate** follows.

114 Apparently White cannot take the Bishop because of the pin on his Rook. But there is a little trick in the position: **1 P x B!, Q x R+; 2 K—Q2, Q x R** (there is nothing better); **3 Q x P+!!, P x Q; 4 B—R6 mate.** The Black Queen has been lured away from the scene of action.

115 **1 Q—KN4!!; Q x Q** (if 1...R x R; 2 Q x Q, R x R+; 3 N x R wins); **2 R x R+, R x R; 3 R x R mate.** The weakness of Black's 1st rank permits this combination. (1 Q—KN4, Q—Q1 also loses to 2 Q x R!, Q x Q; 3 R x R+, Q x R; 4 R x R mate.)

116 White has just snatched a Pawn, thinking that his Knight cannot be captured because of the pin on Black's Queen. Now comes a rude shock! **1...N x N!; 2 B x Q, B—N5+!; 3 Q—Q2, B x Q+; 4 K x Q, K x B.** Black is a Bishop ahead.

117 White has injudiciously snatched a Pawn in the K's Gambit Declined. Retribution is swift: **1...Q—R5+; 2 P—N3** (or if 2 K—K2, Q x KP mate), **Q x KP+; 3 Q—K2, Q x R.**

118 A pin proves decisive: **1...R—Q1!** (threatening 2...B—N6); **2 K—B1, B—N6; 3 R—N1, R x N; 4 K—K1!** (not 4 R x B, R—Q8 mate), **B—R7!; 5 R—R1, R—N7** and Black stays a Bishop ahead.

119 1 ... R—R8+; 2 K—Q2, R—KN8 and White's Bishop is doomed.

120 A neat combination wins material: 1 N x RP!!, K x·N; 2 Q—R5+, K—N1; 3 R—O3! (threatening 4 B—KR3), P —N3; 4 Q x P+, B—N2; 5 R—N3 and mate follows.

121 Morphy (as White) is a Rook behind and finds a clever execution: 1 Q—N4+, K—Q6; 2 Q—K2+, K—B7; 3 P— Q3 dis. ch, K x B; 4 O—O mate!

122 Black (Reshevsky) gets his Queen trapped on an open board! 1 R x N!, P x R; 2 B—N3!

123 White (Bronstein) uses the pin to deliver the *coup de grace*. He ignores his attacked Queen and continues. I B —R6!!, N x Q; 2 B x P+, K—N1; 3 B x N dis. ch B—N4; 4 R x B mate.

124 White's 1st rank is undefended, and Black exploits it quickly: 1 ... B—N4!!; 2 P x B, Q—Q8 mate.

125 White's 1st rank is again undefended: 1 ... B—Q5!; 2 Q x B, Q x B mate.

126 Black wins a Pawn by a deflecting maneuver: 1 ... N x P; 2 N x N, Q x B.

127 Black wins with the help of a finesse: 1 ... B—R7+! (not 1 ... R—R8 ??; 2 K x R, Q—R5 ; 3 Q—R3!); 2 K—R1, B—N6 dis. ch!!; 3 K—N1, R—R8+ (at last); 4 K x R, Q—R5+; 5 K—N1, Q—R7 mate.

128 A clever double attack lurks in the position: 1 Q—K5!! and Black is defenseless against the threats of 2 Q—K8 (... R x Q; 3 R x R mate) OR 2 Q x R.

129 Black's Queen is lost due to a curious discovered attack theme: 1 R—R1, Q—N6; 2 B—B2, Q—N5; 3 R—R4, Q x NP (finally this is forced!); 4 B—R7+, K x R; 5 Q x Q and wins.

130 A deflecting maneuver is decisive: 1 R x R, Q x R; 2 R— K8 , R x R (if 2 ... K—R2; 3 R x R, Q x Q; 4 R x Q); 3 Q x Q+ wins the ensuing endgame.

131 1 R x P+!, K x R; 2 Q—R5+, K—N1; 3 Q—B7+, K—R1; 4 Q x P mate.

132 The awkward position of White's King leads to material loss. 1 . . . Q x Q; 2 N x Q, R—N4!! (with the double threat of 3 R x P mate and/or R x N.); 3 N—B3, R x P+; 4 N—R2 B—B2 and Black wins the pinned Knight.

133 A deflecting maneuver gains Black a piece. 1 . . . P—B6!!; 2 Q x Q (if 2 P x P, Q x N; and on 2 B x P??, Q x Q), P x Q; 3 B x P, P x N; 4 B x P, P—B3. White does not have enough Pawns for his piece.

134 Black is overwhelmingly behind in material, but a pinning tactic leads to victory. 1 . . . Q—B8+!; 2 R—N1, N—N 6+!!; 3 P x N (forced) Q—R6 mate.

135 Black wins with a deflecting maneuver. 1 . . . Q—K4!!; 2 R—Q1 (if 2 Q x Q, N—Q6+; 3 K—N1, R x R mate), Q x N and wins a piece.

136 A series of checks leads to the win of Black's undefended Bishop. 1 R—B8+, R x R; 2 Q x R+, Q—B1; 3 Q—K6+, Q—B2; 4 Q x B.

137 Black's Queen is "overworked" and pinned. 1 B—B6!!, Q x Q; 2 R x B mate. An elegant Evans combination.

138 A sly pin is uncovered by White's key move. 1 P—B4!, **Black Resigns.** He has no defense against either 2 P x B or B x N+.

139 1 R—R7, R—K1 (forced, to prevent 2 R—R8+); 2 P— Q7, R—K2 (again forced); 3 P—Q6!, R x P; 4 R—R8 mate. It is amazing that White can find such a beautiful combination with few pieces left on the board.

140 World-champion Botvinnik proceeds to prove that White's first rank is weak. 1 . . . QR—N1!; 2 Q—Q6, Q x R+!!; 3 K x Q, R—N8+; 4 K—K2, R—B7 mate.

141 Black is an exchange behind, but a sacrificial orgy based upon the pin motif is decisive. 1 . . . N—N6+!; 2 P x N (no better is 2 Q x N, R x Q; 3 P x R, Q—K7), Q—R5+!!; 4 P x Q, R—R6 mate!

142 This has overtones of the smothered mate theme. 1 . . . N— N5! (threatening 2 . . . Q x P mate); 2 R x N (2 Q x Q?,

N—B7 mate), **Q x R** and Black wins material, still remaining with a powerful attack.

143 Black relies on the motif of discovered attack. 1 ... R x B+; 2 K x R, B—Q6+; 3 K—any, Q x Q.

144 A pin regains White's piece with interest. 1 R x N!, R x Q; 2 R x Q, B—Q2; 3 N—N7, and White comes out of the complications at least a piece ahead!

145 Black's undefended last rank allows a familiar finish. 1 B x P!, Q x B; 2 Q—Q8 mate.

146 A forking idea wins White a piece. 1 N—B3!, Q—Q3 (forced); 2 N—K4, Q—any; 3 B x B.

147 A pin saves everything. White sacrifices his Queen – for a slight consideration. 1 Q x P+!!, R x Q; 2 R—K8 mate!

148 The theme is interference or deflection. 1 ... R—Q6!!; 2 B x Q, Q—B6+; 3 R—N2, Q x R mate.

149 A Knight sacrifice leads to victory. 1 ... N—R6+, 2 P x N, Q x P+; 4 K—R1, Q x P mate.

150 Another variation on a theme: smothered mate. 1 ... Q—N8+!; 2 R x Q, N—B7+; 3 K—N2, B—R6 mate.

151 White's weak 1st rank allows a winning combination. 1 ... B—R3!!; 2 B x B, Q—B7+; 3 K—R1, Q—B8+; 4 R x Q, R x R mate.

152 A cute fork wins White a piece. 1 R x N!, Q x R; 2 Q x R+!!, K x Q; 3 N—N6+ *(der punkt!)*, K—any; 4 N x Q.

153 Black's lack of development is punished. 1 N—QN5! (threatening 2 N—B7), R—B1; 2 N—B7, R—N1; 3 N x KP, Q—R4+; 4 P—QN4 wins material.

154 A sly move traps Black's awkwardly placed Queen: 1 B—R5!

155 A Queen sacrifice leaves Black helpless. 1 Q x P+!!, K x Q; 2 B—B6+, K—N1; 3 R—R4, and Black is helpless against the threat of 4 R—R8 mate.

156 Black has better than the simple N x KP: 1 ... N—K6!!; 2 P x N, Q—R5+; 3 P—N3, Q x P mate.

157 A delightful fork wins White's Queen. 1 ... B x P+!!; 2

K x B (2 Q x B loses also to N—Q6+), N x P+; 3 K—any, N x Q.

158 A pin wins White's Queen: 1 ... Q—R5+!!; 2 K—any, Q x Q.

159 Black wins a piece with a forking maneuver. 1 ... R—N5!; 2 Q x BP, B—Q2; 3 Q—B3, R x B.

160 A clearance maneuver wins: 1 Q—R8+, K—R2; 2 Q—R 8+!!, N x Q; 3 R—N7 mate.

161 Black is punished for Pawn grabbing with his Queen. 1 N —R4, and Black's Queen is trapped!

162 1 P—B6!, P x P; 2 B x P, and the fork wins material.

163 A stock Queen sacrifice. 1 Q x P+!, K x Q; 2 R—R3+, K—N1; 3 R—R8 mate.

GAME SECTION

INDEX TO GAMES

Game Number	Players	Year	Opening
1	Anderssen vs. Kieseritzky	1851	King's Gambit
2	Anderssen vs. Dufresne	1853	Evans Gambit
3	Em. Lasker vs. Napier	1904	Sicilian Defense
4	Bogoljubow vs. Alekhine	1922	Dutch Defense
5	Reti vs. Alekhine	1925	King's Fianchetto
6	Alekhine vs. Pomar	1944	Ruy Lopez
7	Evans vs. Pilnick	1946	French Defense
8	Euwe vs. Steiner	1946	Nimzo-Indian Defense
9	Reshevsky vs. Stahlberg	1947	Catalan System
10	Evans vs. Sandrin	1948	Queen's Indian
11	Evans vs. Opsahl	1950	Queen's Gambit
12	Najdorf vs. Kramer	1950	Catalan System
13	Adams vs. Evans	1951	Sicilian Defense
14	Euwe vs. Evans	1951	Queen's Indian
15	Evans vs. Santasiere	1951	Nimzo-Indian Defense
16	Prins and Evans vs. Reshevsky and Horowitz	1951	Sicilian Defense

No. 1
ANDERSSEN vs. KIESERITZKY
King's Bishop Gambit
London, 1951
"The Immortal Game"

White	Black
1 P—K4	P—K4
2 P—KB4	P x P
3 B—B4	P—QN4?

This ruins the Pawn structure and is contrary to modern prin-

ciples, but Black hardly knew it. If he had known, he would
have played 2 . . . P—Q4.

4	B x P	Q—R5ch
5	K—B1	N—KB3
6	N—KB3	Q—R3
7	P—Q3	N—R4
8	N—R4	P—QB3
9	N—B5	Q—N4
10	P—KN4	N—B3
11	R—N1!	P x B

Very obliging. It is difficult to evaluate this game except in an
historical sense since modern theory is relatively so far advanced that both attack and defense seem ludicrous to us today.

12	P—KR4	Q—N3
13	P—R5	Q—N4
14	Q—B3	N—N1

To give the Queen escape squares after 15 B x P. Black is bot-
tling himself up.

15	B x P	Q—B3
16	N—B3	B—B4
17	N—Q5	Q x P

There is nothing better. Now follow a deep and original combination. White sacrifices the kitchen sink!

Diagram 164

18 **B—Q6!**	**B x R**

If 18 . . . Q x Rch; 19 K—K2, Q x R; 20 N x Pch, K—Q1; 21 B —B7 mate.

19 **P—K5!**	**Q x Rch**
20 **K—K2**	**N—QR3**
21 **N x Pch**	**K—Q1**

Now follows mate in two.

Diagram 165

22 **Q—B6ch!!**	**N x Q**
23 **B—K7 mate**	

More pieces have never been successfully sacrificed in one game. White gave up a Bishop, two Rooks and a Queen!

No. 2

ANDERSSEN vs. DUFRESNE
Evans Gambit
Berlin, 1853
"The Evergreen Game"

White	Black
1 P—K4	P—K4
2 N—KB3	N—QB3
3 B—B4	B—B4
4 P—QN4	. . . .

The Evans Gambit. Black can safely decline, if he so chooses, by 4 . . . B—N3.

4	. . . .	B x P
5	P—B3	B—R4
6	P—Q4	P x P

Much better is 6 . . . P—Q3, and if 7 O—O, B—N3!—Lasker's Defense, discovered many years after this game.

7	O—O	P—Q6

Weak. Better is 7 . . . B—N3; 8 P x P, P—Q3 with equal chances.

8	Q—N3	Q—B3
9	P—K5	Q—N3
10	R—K1	KN—K2
11	B—R3	P—N4?

11 . . . O—O followed by rapid development is imperative. Black's King must not linger in the center.

12	Q x P	R—QN1
13	Q—R4	B—N3
14	QN—Q2	. . . .

Bringing his pieces out. Anderssen was the first pre-Morphyite who understood the value of development. Now the Q R is free to move.

14	. . . .	B—N2
15	N—K4	Q—B4
16	B x P	Q—R4

Black meanwhile wastes millions of tempi moving his Queen.

17	N—B6ch!	P x N
18	P x P	R—N1
19	QR—Q1!	. . . .

A very subtle move. Black misses the point.

19	. . . .	Q x N?

Black's co-operation allows the combination, luckily for us! True, his position is decidedly inferior despite the extra piece, but after 19 . . . Q—R6! White's task would have been much more difficult.

Diagram 166

20	R x N ch!	N x R
21	Q x P ch!!	K x Q
22	B—B5 ch	K—K1
23	B—Q7 ch	K—Q1
24	B x N mate	

The next three games may not match these in sparkle, but at least the loser plays well and puts up the best resistance. It is much more difficult to get away with a brilliancy nowadays because the general level of chess strength has so risen that every player has a knowledge of general principles; and it is not easy to sacrifice pieces against a sound development and a healthy Pawn bulwark.

Often there is more satisfaction derived from a finely played lost game than from any number of wins secured through errors of an opponent. True, the tournament player wants to win—but from an adversary worthy of his steel.

Surely it is no exaggeration to say that this game "is one of the most beautiful, most profound, most exciting, and most difficult in the whole literature of chess." Napier, *the loser,* considered it the best game that he had ever played!

No. 3

EM. LASKER vs NAPIER
Sicilian Defense
Cambridge Springs, 1904

	White	Black
1	P—K4	P—QB4
2	N—QB3	N—QB3
3	N—B3	P—KN3
4	P—Q4	P x P
5	N x P	B—N2
6	B—K3	P—Q3
7	P—KR3	N—B3
8	P—KN4	....

A premature attack which Lasker essays for divers psychological reasons.

8	....	O—O
9	P—N5	N—K1
10	P—KR4	N—B2
11	P—B4	P—K4!
12	KN—K2	P—Q4!?

Risky. 12 ... B—N5 gives Black the better game. Black now does not profit from open lines.

| 13 | KP x P | N—Q5! |
| 14 | N x N! | N x P |

Not 15 N x N?, P x N!; 16 B x P, Q x N; 17 B x B, Q x R; 18 B x R, Q x Pch.

15	N—B5!!	N x N!
16	Q x Q	R x Q
17	N—K7ch	....

If 17 N x B, N—Q4; 18 B—Q2, P x P.

| 17 | .... | K—R1! |

Not 17 ... K—B1?; 18 B—B5, N—K5; 19 B—QR3. We can realize the depth of Black's defense only when we note that his opponent is now seemingly without a satisfactory continuation; for if 18 P x N, P x P; 19 B—Q4, B x B; 20 P x B, R—K1! with a winning game.

Diagram 167

18	P—R5!!	R—K1!
19	B—B5	NP x P
20	B—B4!!	....

20 P x N, B—B1; 21 B—N5, R x N; 22 B x R, B x B is in Black's favor.

20	....	P x P!!
21	B x BP!	N—K5!!
22	B x R	B x P
23	QR—N1	B—B6ch
24	K—B1	B—KN5!

Although Black is a Rook down, he has a bewildering array of threats. But a Rook is a Rook!

25	KB x P!	B x B
26	R x B!	N—N6ch
27	K—N2	N x R
28	R x P	P—R4
29	R—N3!	B—N2
30	R—KR3	N—N6
31	K—B3	R—R3
32	K x P	N—K7ch
33	K—B5	N—B6

| 34 | P—R3 | N—R5 |
| 35 | B—K3 | Resigns |

For 36 P—N6 wins easily.

In my opinion Alexander Alekhine was the greatest chess genius the world has ever known, or is likely to know for a long time to come. His last days were spent in Madrid in voluntary exile. His games live on to charm the hearts of men. Something of the turbulence and storm of his life is reflected in the mirror of the 64 squares.

No. 4
BOGOLJUBOW vs. ALEKHINE
Dutch Defense
Hastings, 1922

	White	Black
1	P—Q4	P—KB4
2	P—QB4	N—KB3
3	P—KN3	P—K3
4	B—N2	B—N5ch
5	B—Q2	B x Bch
6	N x B	....

6 Q x B followed by N—QB3 is better.

6	....	N—B3
7	KN—B3	O—O
8	O—O	P—Q3
9	Q—N3	K—R1
10	Q—B3	P—K4!
11	P—K3	P—QR4!
12	P—N3	Q—K1!
13	P—QR3	Q—R4!
14	P—KR4	....

Not 14 P x P, P x P; 15 N x P?, N x N; 16 Q x N, N—N5 winning outright.

14	....	N—KN5
15	N—N5	B—Q2

16	P—B3	N—B3
17	P—B4	....

17 ... P—B5! was threatened, so White blocks the position.

17	....	P—K5
18	KR—Q1	P—R3
19	N—R3	P—Q4!
20	N—B1	N—K2
21	P—R4	N—B3!
22	R—Q2	N—QN5
23	B—R1	Q—K1!
24	R—KN2	P x P
25	P x P	B x P
26	N—B2	B—Q2
27	N—Q2	P—QN4!
28	N—Q1	N—Q6!

Preparing the ensuing combination.

29	R x P	P—N5!
30	R x R	P x Q!
31	R x Q	....

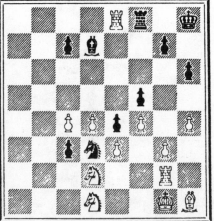

Diagram 168

If Black takes the Rook he loses his passed Pawn.

31	....	P—B7!!

The point! White cannot prevent this Pawn from queening.

32	R x Rch	K—R2
33	N—B2	P—B8=Qch
34	N—B1	N—K8!

Threatening . . . N—B6 mate!

35	R—R2	Q x BP

Threatening 36 . . . B—N4.

36	R—QN8	B—N4
37	R x B	Q x R
38	P—N4	N—B6ch!
39	B x N	P x B
40	P x P	Q—K7!!
41	P—Q5	K—N1!
42	P—R5	K—R2
43	P—K4	N x KP
44	N x N	Q x N
45	P—Q6	P x P
46	P—B6	P x P
47	R—Q2	Q—K7!
48	R x Q	P x R
49	K—B2	P x N = Qch
50	K x Q	K—N2
51	K—B2	K—B2
52	K—K3	K—K3
53	K—K4	P—Q4ch

Resigns

Alekhine here outplays Reti, the father of the hypermodern school. I consider this the most brilliant game of the modern era.

No. 5

RETI vs. ALEKHINE
King's Fianchetto
Baden-Baden, 1925

White	Black
1 P—KN3	P—K4

2	N—KB3	P—K5
3	N—Q4	P—Q4
4	P—Q3	P x P
5	Q x P	N—KB3
6	B—N2	B—N5ch
7	B—Q2	B x Bch
8	N x B	O—O
9	P—QB4!	N—R3
10	P x P	N—QN5
11	Q—B4	QN x QP
12	QN—N3	P—B3
13	O—O	R—K1
14	KR—Q1	B—N5
15	R—Q2	Q—B1
16	N—QB5	B—R6!
17	B—B3	B—N5
18	B—N2	B—R6

Black, having a slightly inferior position, is content with a draw by repetition of moves.

19	B—B3	B—N5
20	B—R1	....

Playing for the win and allowing Black the opportunity of an enterprising counterattack.

20	....	P—KR4!
21	P—QN4	P—QR3
22	R—QB1	P—R5
23	P—R4	P x P
24	RP x P	Q—B2
25	P—N5	RP x P
26	P x P	R—K6!!!

An incredible move! If now 27 P x R?, Q x Pch; 28 K—B1 or B—N2, N x P wins.

27	N—B3	P x P
28	Q x P	N—B6!
29	Q x P	....

After 29 Q—B4, P—QN4;! is decisive.

29 ....   Q x Q

   If 29 . . . N x Pch; 30 R x N!, Q x Q; 31 R x R!

30 N x Q   N x Pch

31 K—R2   ....

   Or 31 K—B1, N x Pch; 32 P x N, B x N; 33 B x B, R x Bch; 34 K—N2, R(R1)—R6; 35 R—Q8ch, K—R2; 36 R—R1 ch, K —N3; 37 R—R3, R(B6)=QN6! and wins. (Alekhine.)

Diagram 169

31 ....   N—K5!

32 R—B4!   ....

   Relatively best. The Rook is still taboo as 32 P x R?, N(K5) x R! wins the exchange. (33 N x N, N x R.)

32 ....   N x BP

   If 32 . . . N x R; 33 N x N!

33 B—N2   B—K3!

34 R(B4)—B2   N—N5ch

35 K—R3   ....

   Not 35 K—R1, R—R8ch. White's moves are peculiarly forced.

35 ....   N—K4 dis ch

36 K—R2   R x N!

37 R x N   N—N5ch

38 K—R3   N—K6 dis ch

39	K—R2	N x R
40	B x R	N—Q5

If now 41 R—K3(B2), then ... N x Bch; 42 R x N, B—Q4! (the final point!) winning a piece. (Alekhine.) Therefore ... White resigns.

No. 6

ALEKHINE vs. POMAR
Ruy Lopez
Gijon, 1944

	White	Black
1	P—K4	P—K4
2	N—KB3	N—QB3
3	B—N5	P—QR3
4	B—R4	N—B3
5	O—O	P—Q3

The Steinitz Defense Deferred. 5 ... B—K2 or ... N x P are also good.

6	P—B3	B—N5

Premature. Black must consolidate before launching a counterattack, and for this reason the solid ... B—Q2 is preferable.

7	P—Q4	P—QN4
8	B—N3	B—K2
9	B—K3	O—O

Strict development. The Pawn is poison: 9 ... N x KP?; 10 B—Q5, and White wins a piece — a standard trap.

10	QN—Q2	R—K1

Weakening the King Bishop Pawn. Better is 10 ... P x P; 11 P x P, P—Q4!; 12 P—K5, N—K5!

11	P—KR3	....

Known as "putting the question to the Bishop." In master play the preservation of the "two Bishops" is axiomatic, thus 11 ... Bx N is unthinkable. The main point is that the Bishop must either relinquish the pin or the QB1—KR6 diagonal. The method that Black actually chooses leaves it more or less out of play.

| 11 | .... | B—R4 |

11 ... B—Q2 is preferable.

| 12 | P—Q5 | .... |

Alekhine decides to play for a King-side attack and prepares it by closing the center.

| 12 | .... | N—R4 |
| 13 | B—B2 | R—QB1 |

More to the point is 13 ... P—B4. No time should be lost in countering White's King-side attack with a Queen-side offensive.

| 14 | P—QR4 | .... |

With typical elasticity of outlook Alekhine keeps the situation fluid on both flanks.

14	....	P—B4
15	P x P	P x P
16	P—KN4	B—N3
17	N—R4	N—Q2

He rejects the dubious win of a Pawn by 17 .... B x P; 18 B x B, N x B; 19 N x N, B x N; 20 R x N!, Q x R; 21 N x QP, etc.

| 18 | N—B5 | B x N |

Welcoming the chance to get rid of his useless Bishop, but the move also has its drawbacks: it permits White to open lines for his attack.

| 19 | NP x N | B—N4 |

According to general principles, when defending, exchange pieces!

| 20 | Q—K2 | .... |

All attempts at winning two pieces for a Rook fail, e.g., 20 R x N, B x B!, or if 20 B x B, Q x Bch foils White's scheme.

| 20 | .... | P—B5 |
| 21 | K—R1 | .... |

Finally threatening B x B. The position is difficult to appraise. Black has the better long-range prospects but White, on the

other hand, has a base of operations on his open King's Knight
file. All in all, Black has emerged from the opening with a
creditable position.

| 21 | .... | R—R1 |

Defending against the threat and occupying the open Queen
Rook file — an important motif.

22	R—KN1	B x B
23	Q x B	Q—B3
24	R—N4	K—R1

Young Pomar is overcautious because he has too much respect for Alekhine's attacking prowess. He is better advised
to continue with 24 . . . N—N2, and if 25 QR—KN1, K—R1.

| 25 | QR—KN1 | R—KN1 |

Again unnecessary. Pomar's caution gets him in hot water.

| 26 | N—B3 | N—N2 |
| 27 | R—R4 | R—R3? |

Since White threatens nothing, the more aggressive 27 . . . .
R—R7 should be preferred.

| 28 | Q—N5 | .... |

Meancing a break-through by 29 R x Pch!, K x R; 30 Q—
R5ch, Q—R3; 31 N—N5 ch, K—R1; 32 N x Pch, K—R2; 33 N x
Q, etc.

| 28 | .... | N—Q1! |

The best defense. Not 28 . . . P—R3; 29 Q—R5 threatening
N—R2 followed by N—N4 and the sacrifice.

| 29 | Q—R5 | N—B1 |
| 30 | N—R2 | P—N3 |

Ordinarily weaknesses should be avoided when defending,
but this one works out well. 29 . . . Q—K2; 30 N—N4, P—B3!
followed by a Queen-side counterattack, however, is even
better.

| 31 | Q—R6 | Q—N2 |

In the face of an onslaught that would unnerve many a
seasoned defender, young Pomar plays with the grace of a
mature master.

| 32 | N—N4 | P—B3! |

Diagram 170

Alekhine is now hard pressed to find a continuation. His attack has been repulsed and his Rook stands out of play on R4; moreover, Black threatens ... P—KN4.

33	P x P	Q x P
34	Q—K3	....

White has found a way to sustain the initiative. Now he intends 35 R—R6.

| 34 | .... | Q—N4 |

Impatient to exchange.

35	R—R6	Q x Q
36	P x Q	N—Q2!
37	R—KB1	....

Not 37 N x BP, R x Rch; 38 K x R, N—B1 with the double threat of 39 ... K—N2 or 39 ... R—R8ch followed by ... R—QB8.

| 37 | .... | R—R7 |

Even stronger is 37 ... N—B2; 38 R—R5, R—N3; 39 R(R5) —B5, R—R7! with victory in sight.

38	N x BP	N x N
39	R(R6) x N	R x P
40	B—Q1	R(1)—N7

Threatening mate in two.

41	B—B3	R—N6
42	B—N4	R(6)—N7
43	R—R1!?	....

Spurning the repetition by 43 B—B3. Although his King is more exposed, Alekhine is willing to speculate. Now comes a seesaw battle.

| 43 | .... | R—R7ch |
| 44 | K—N1 | R(R7)—N7ch |

Avoiding 44 ... R(N7)—N7ch; 45 K—B1, R x B; 46 P x R, R—R8ch; 47 K—B2, R x R; 48 R—B8ch, K—N2; 49 R x N, R—R7ch; 50 K—B3, R—B7 with a draw in sight.

| 45 | K—B1 | .... |

Still out to win. 45 K—R1 draws easily.

| 45 | .... | R—KR7 |

Threatening 46 ... R—R8 mate.

| 46 | K—K1? | .... |

But here Alekhine definitely overreaches himself. K—N1 is essential.

| 46 | .... | P—N5? |

And Pomar, in his turn, misses a chance for immortality. The win is 46 ... N—N2! and White is defenseless against 47 ... N—B4 followed by ... N—Q6ch.

| 47 | P x P | P—B6 |
| 48 | R—QB1 | .... |

In order to prevent ... P—B7.

| 48 | .... | P—R4 |

To free the Knight. On 48 ... P—B7 White had concocted the ingenious 49 R—B2, R—R8ch; 50 K—Q2 (not 50 R—B1, R x Rch; 51 K x R, R—N8), R—Q8 ch!; 51 K—B3!! (not 51 R x R?, P x R=Qch; 52 K x Q, R x R wins), and wins!

| 49 | B—Q1 | .... |

Not 49 B x P, R—R8ch; 50 R—B1, R x RP; 51 B—B3, N—B2 and wins.

| 49 | .... | K—N2 |
| 50 | R—B1 | P—B7 |

51	B—K2	N—B2
52	K—Q2	R x NP
53	R x P	N—N4
54	R—QB7ch	K—N3
55	K—B3	R—R5

Not 55 ... R x KP??; 56 B—Q3.

| 56 | B—N5? | .... |

Another winning try which should lead to a loss. 56 K—N3 should be good enough for a draw.

56	....	N x Pch!
57	K—N3	R(5)—R7!
58	R—N1ch	....

Alekhine doubtlessly intended 58 B—Q3 but overlooked 58 ... R(KR7)—N7 mate in his calculations. He is on the ropes again.

58	....	K—R3
59	R—N1	R(QR7)—Q7
60	B—Q7	R x QP

White is now dead lost...

| 61 | K—B4 | .... |

Diagram 171

| 61 | .... | R—B7ch? |

... but Black goes astray at the last moment. Correct is 61

...R(4)—Q7 (threatening 62...R—B7ch winning a Rook)
followed by...P—Q4ch and the win is a mere matter of technique. The vicissitudes in this ending are truly amazing!

62	K x R	R x R
63	K x N	R x B
64	P—R4	P—Q4ch

Pomar returns the Pawn advantage in order to force a sure
draw. (White's pieces are too well posted for there to be any
question of a win.) He was justifiably frightened of his re-
nowned opponent throughout the game and threw away at
least two clear wins in the ending. There is more to a game
of chess than skill, there is an enormous amount of psychological tension; and a master must soon learn that one cannot live
with fear.

65	K x P	R—K2ch
66	K—B5	....

Still trying! 66 K x P, R x P resolves into an elementary
draw.

66	....	R x P
67	R—N6ch	K—R2
68	R—Q6	R—K5
69	R—Q7ch	K—R3

One can almost sense the World Champion's fierce desire
to win at all costs. This attempt to exert mind over matter is
typical of all Alekhine's tournament games.

70	R—Q6ch	K—R2
71	R—Q7ch	K—R3

Drawn

Incidentally, Pomar was thirteen years old when this game
was played!

No. 7

EVANS vs. C. PILNICK
French Defense

Marshall Chess Club Championship, 1946

	White	Black
1	P—K4	P—K3
2	P—Q4	P—Q4
3	N—QB3	N—KB3
4	B—N5	B—K2
5	B x N	....

It is not customary to relinquish the two Bishops without being provoked, but White chose this little-known variation because his standing in the tournament forced him to try to win at all costs.

5	....	BxB
6	P—K5	B—K2
7	Q—N4	O—O!

Castling into it! But Black has nothing to fear. He has made no weaknesses, lost no tempi, therefore he goes about completing his development in the calm assurance that White's premature attack should be repulsed. And he is right.

| 8 | O—O—O | P—QB4 |
| 9 | P—KR4 | .... |

White is committed to this violent course since he cannot stop to defend on the Queen side.

| 9 | .... | P x P |
| 10 | QN—K2 | .... |

Black's reaction has been exemplary. Not 10 R x P, N—QB3, developing with tempo and winning the King Pawn.

10	....	N—B3
11	P—KB4	Q—R4
12	K—N1	P—Q6!

The Pawn was indefensible in any event, so White is forced to accept it in such a manner that he gets in the way of his own pieces.

| 13 | P x P | .... |

Not 13 R x P?, Q—K8ch and 14 ... Q x B.

| 13 | .... | B—Q2 |
| 14 | R—R3 | QR—B1 |

But here ... P—KB4! is called for and White's attack comes to an abrupt standstill. Pilnick becomes too intent on his own counterattack, a fault against which we must be on guard.

15	R—N3	P—KN3
16	P—Q4	P—QN4
17	P—R5	N—N5

Inducing a weakness in White's King position. Now the race is to get there "fustest with the mostest."

18	P—R3	N—B3
19	P x P	BP x P
20	N—QB3!	....

To untangle the pieces. At this point White had to envisage the sacrificial combination which he essays at his twenty-fourth turn. In executing his plans, White must forego the necessary evil of permitting Black to continue his counterattack with gain of time by attacking the Knight.

20	....	P—N5
21	B—Q3	....

Whenever possible make a threat with gain of time. Now 21.... P x N is impossible in view of B x P! Black must stop to defend.

21	....	B—K1

Better is 21 ... R—B4!

22	N—B3!!	....

The finest move in the whole game.

22	....	P x P

The defense with 22 ... R—B4 fails because of 23 B x R, KP x B; 24 Q x P! The main variation runs: 22 ... P x N; 23 Q x KPch, B—B2; 24 B x P!! and we enter the same analysis starting from Diagram 172, with the difference that Black is a Knight ahead and his Pawn is on B6 instead of R6.

23	Q x KPch	B—B2
24	B x P!!	....
24	....	P x P

Admirable nonchalance! The main variation is the accept-

Diagram 172

ance of the Queen, e.g., 24...B x Q; 25 B x Pch, K—R1 (if 25...K—B2; 26 B—N6ch, K—N2; 27 B—K8ch!, K—R1; 28 R—R1 mate; or 25...K x B; 26 R—R1 mate); 26 R—R1!, R xP! (forced); 27 B—B2 dis ch, B—R5; 28 N x B with an easy win.

25	B x Pch	K—R1
26	Q—R6	Q—R8ch

Black is left with a few spite checks.

27	K—B2	P—N8=Qch
28	R x Q	N—N5ch
29	K—Q1	Resigns

His checks have petered out and mate cannot be averted.

No. 8

EUWE vs. STEINER
Nimzo-Indian Defense
Groningen, 1946

	White	Black
1	P—Q4	N—KB3
2	P—QB4	P—K3
3	N—QB3	B—N5
4	P—K3	O—O

More noncommittal than either ... P—Q4 or ... P—B4; but
the tendency of modern play is to delay the battle until late
in the middle game.

5	B—Q3	....

5 N—K2 is sharper.

5	....	P—Q4
6	P—QR3	B x Nch

Good — and bad! In the two previous games we noticed the
bitter reluctance to part with the two Bishops, and here, too,
White goes out of his way to obtain them. Black is very obliging. A strong alternative to the text is 6 ... P x P; 7 B x P,
B—Q3 followed by ... P—K4 as soon as possible.

7	P x B	QN—Q2
8	P x P	....

Dissolving the doubled Pawns.

8	....	P x P
9	N—K2	....

The customary place for a Knight is B3, but some positions
call for specific measures instead of general principles. The
game is a sharp illustration of the fight for control of the center
in its most elemental form. It has been written that when White
plays 1 P—Q4 his object is to force P—K4 at a favorable
moment. Accordingly, Euwe sees that this Knight belongs on
KN3 where, after P—B3, it helps support the advance of the
King Pawn to K4. Black bends all his efforts to prevent the advance — which is what gives the game its character.

9	....	R—K1
10	O—O	N—B1

10 ... P—B4 is more energetic.

11	P—B3	P—B4
12	N—N3	....

After 12 P x P, Q—R4 Black regains the Pawn with the
upper hand.

12	....	P x P
13	BP x P	P—QR3

Preparing to swap off Euwe's valuable King Bishop after B–Q2 to N4.

14 Q–Q2   . . . .

Not 14 P–K4, P x P; 15 P x P, Q x Pch and wins. White now intends B–N2, protecting his Queen Pawn, followed by a steamroller advance in the center.

14 . . . .   **B–Q2**

There is no good square for the Queen Bishop – Black's "problem child" in the Queen's Gambit.

15 P–K4   **P x P**

16 P–K5, winning a piece, was threatened.

16 P x P   **B–B3**

17 P–Q5   **B–N4**

The idea being that if 18 B x B, Q–N3 ch!; 19 K–R1, Q x B and White is abominably weak on his light-colored squares.

18 B–N2!   . . . .

A superb comeback. But how does he avoid losing a piece after 18 . . . Q–N3ch?

18 . . . .   **Q–N3ch**

19 K–R1   **B x B**

Black's best chance is to go after the piece. Black has made no errors which deserve outright question marks but the strength of the advance has been overwhelming. Steiner's error, if anything, has been passive defense. Specific mistakes can be traced back to the opening; for in master chess, nothing goes unpunished.

Diagram 173

How does White continue? If 20 Q x B, Q x B and Black simply remains a piece ahead.

20 R x N!!   ....

The tactic underlying the strategy. White is essaying a positional combination since at the end he neither wins nor loses material (but Black's Pawn structure is left irremediably weak).

20 ....   **P x R**

Or if 20 ... Q—N4; 21 P—QR4 wins.

21 N—R5!   **R—K4**

Forced. There is no other way to meet the double threat of either Q—R6 or N x Pch.

22	B x R	P x B
23	Q x B	Q—R3
24	Q—R3	....

A comparison of this position with the one after Black's seventeenth move reveals the purpose of the combination: Black's Pawn formation is discombobulated and his King hopelessly exposed.

24	....	R—Q1
25	R—KB1	Q—N4
26	Q—KB3	Q—N3
27	N—N3	R—Q2
28	Q—B3	Q—Q3
29	N—B5	Q—B2
30	Q—N3ch	N—N3

There is nothing for Black to do but grit his teeth and wait. It is just a matter of time.

31	Q—N5	Q—Q1
32	N—R6ch	K—N2
33	R—B6!	....

Also good is 33 N x P.

33	....	Q—R4
34	R—B1	Q x RP

A desperate measure. But 34 ... Q—Q1; 35 N x P is equally hopeless for Black.

35	N—B5ch	K—N1
36	Q—B6	Q—B1
37	R—B1	R—Q1
38	R—B7!	Resigns

Black is helpless against 39 R x BP followed by N—R6ch.

Here is a game from a radio match which should be entitled "getting something out of nothing."

No. 9
RESHEVSKY vs. STAHLBERG
Catalan System
Match: New York vs. Argentina, 1947

	White	Black
1	N—KB3	P—Q4
2	P—KN3	....

Reti's so-called "hypermodern idea." White intends to control the center from the wings rather than occupy it directly with Pawns.

2	....	N—KB3
3	B—N2	P—KN3

Imitation is the most insincere form of flattery. 3 ... B—B4 is perhaps even better.

4	P—Q4	B—N2
5	O—O	O—O
6	P—B4	P—B4

Maintaining the symmetry. If 6 ... P x P; 7N—R3 regains the Pawn.

7	P x BP	P x P

The question is whether or not White can utilize his first move.

8	Q—B2	Q—Q4
9	N—R3	Q x P
10	Q x BP	Q x Q

If 10 ... N—R3; 11 B—K3.

| 11 | N x Q | N—B3 |
| 12 | QN—K5 | .... |

Not just another exchange. White wants to unmask his King Bishop on the long diagonal.

| 12 | .... | N x N |
| 13 | N x N | .... |

That White can win by force from this position is a moot point, but it is difficult indeed to suggest any concrete improvements over Stahlberg's defense.

| 13 | .... | N—K1 |

The best chance is 13...N—N5; 14 N—Q3, N—K4; 15N—B5, N—B5.

| 14 | N—Q3 | N—Q3 |

Once again a mirror image. Can it be that whoever moves wins? Time is a crucial element.

Diagram 174

| 15 | B—N5! | .... |

The initiative of the first move is vital.

| 15 | .... | R—K1 |

Avoiding weaknesses at all cost. Of course not 15... P—K4?; 16 B—K7 wins the exchange. And if 15...P—B3; 16 B—B4 followed by QR—B1 with a Queen-side bind. And finally, if Black tries to maintain the symmetry by 15...B—

N5; 16 B x P, B x P; 17 B x N, B x N; 18 B x R, B x R; 19 B x B, B x B; 20 K x B, K x B; 21 R—QB1, he cannot prevent the incursion of the Rook to the seventh rank — but Black may hold the draw.

16	QR—B1	P—KR3
17	B—K3	....

The Bishops rake the Queen side.

17	....	B—B4
18	R—B7	B x N

This seems wrong on principle, but there is hardly anything better. If 18 . . . QR—B1; 19 KR—B1, R x R; 20 R x R, R—QB1; 21 R x R, B x R; 22 B x QRP and White wins.

19	P x B	QR—B1

19 . . . B x P is better.

20	KR—B1	R x R
21	R x R	B x P
22	B x NP	B—B3
23	B—B6	R—N1

Black must lose a Pawn by force, but he can put up a stronger resistance with 23 . . . R—QB1; 24 R x R, N x R; 25 B x KRP, N—N3, though he should still lose.

24	B x QRP	R—N8ch
25	K—N2	R—QR8
26	P—QR4	....

The forward-march of this Rook Pawn must be carefully conducted. Reshevsky chaperones it to the queening square.

26	....	N—B4
27	B—N6	B—Q5
28	P—R5	B—B6
29	R—R7	N—Q5
30	B—K4	N—N6
31	P—R6	B—Q5
32	B x B	N x B
33	R—Q7	P—B4
34	B—Q5ch	Resigns

A superb example of economical technique by Reshevsky, who utilized the initiative of the first move with demoniacal persistence. If now 34 . . . P—K3; 35 P—R7 wins the exchange: 35 . . . P x B; 36 R—Q8ch, K—B2; 37 P—R8=Q, R x Q; 38 R x R, etc.

No. 10

EVANS vs. SANDRIN
Queen's Indian Defense
United States Championship, 1948

White	Black
1 P—Q4	N—KB3
2 P—QB4	P—K3
3 N—KB3	P—QN3

The Queen's Indian Defense. At this point Black may transpose into the Queen's Gambit Declined by . . . P—Q4.

| 4 P—KN3 | . . . . |

4 N—B3, B—N2; 5 Q—B2, B—N5 leads to equality. The fianchetto of the White Bishop neutralizes the power of Black's on the long diagonal.

4	B—N2
5 B—N2	B—K2
6 O—O	O—O
7 Q—B2	. . . .

The usual — and stronger — move is N—B3, but the text was played to avoid stereotyped variations. The Queen eyes the K4 square.

| 7 . . . . | Q—B1 |

A solid reply. An attempt to capitalize on White's last move is 7 . . . N—B3 or . . . P—B4 with sharp play. The chances are equal.

| 8 N—B3 | . . . . |

As in the preceding game, the struggle rages around White's K4.

| 8 . . . . | P—B4? |

In the Queen's Indian Defense this move is always desirable

but always critical when White has the possibility of P—Q5. Black should meet the threat of P—K4 by . . . P—Q4. (Kmoch.)

| 9 | P—Q5! | . . . . |

After which Black is cramped.

| 9 | . . . . | P x P |
| 10 | P x P | P—Q3 |

As always, strategy is supplemented by tactics; in this case Black found that he could not play 10 . . . N x P because of 11 N x N, B x N; 12 N—N5! winning the exchange.

| 11 | P—K4 | . . . . |

The next phase of the game requires patience and steadiness. White's objective is to apply pressure and keep Black cramped so that ultimately he will be powerless to prevent P—K5.

11	. . . .	QN—Q2
12	B—B4	R—K1
13	KR—K1	. . . .

The kind of move that has been ascribed to "positional instinct." Actually it is a logical developing move in accord with the general principle that Rooks should be placed on open files.

| 13 | . . . . | P—QR3 |

Striving for counterplay.

| 14 | QR—Q1 | B—KB1 |
| 15 | B—R3 | . . . . |

Now the positional pressure becomes more direct: the text prepares P—K5.

| 15 | . . . . | Q—N1 |

Getting out of the pin.

| 16 | B—N5 | P—R3 |

Forced to do something, Black makes a weakness. Having provoked . . . P—KR3, which adds substantially to the efficiency of a possible N—KR4—B5 maneuver, the Bishop returns to its original square awaiting deployment elsewhere.

| 17 | B—QB1 | P—QN4 |
| 18 | N—KR4 | P—B5 |

The best chance.

| 19 | B—B1 | . . . . |

Consolidating against the . . . N—B4—Q6 maneuver. Now that Black has committed himself on the Queen side, White's King Bishop comes back into play.

| 19 | . . . . | Q—B2 |
| 20 | P—B3 | QR—B1 |

White's advantage is in space. His problem is to poise his pieces for the break-through.

| 21 | B—K3 | P—N3 |
| 22 | B—Q4 | . . . . |

Was ever a Bishop on a happier square?

| 22 | . . . . | B—N2 |
| 23 | B—R3 | . . . . |

Back again!

| 23 | . . . . | R—N1 |
| 24 | Q—B2 | R—K2 |

An error which allows a pretty combination. Since Black has a bad game anyway, it is not clear how he could improve his position. One can only blame the text move for speeding defeat.

Diagram 175

25 P—K5!! . . . .

Owing to a number of tactical circumstances, this strategical break-through decides the game at a moment when the move hardly looks playable. (Kmoch.)

| 25 | .... | P x P |

He must take—and yet he cannot take! On 25...N x KP; 26 B—N6 wins the Queen. If 25...N—K1; 26 P—K6! decides.

| 26 | B—R7! | .... |

The point. White threatens both 27 P—Q6 and B x R.

| 26 | .... | Q—Q3 |
| 27 | B x R | Q x B |

The win is technically difficult for White since Black holds two Bishops and a sound Pawn for the exchange. White's slight material advantage is supplemented by his passed Pawn. Together, these two factors are conclusive.

| 28 | P—Q6 | R—K1 |
| 29 | N—K4 | .... |

Each simplification brings White nearer his goal.

29	....	R—Q1
30	N x Nch	N x N
31	Q—B5	....

Threatening Q—B7.

| 31 | .... | P—N4 |

Yielding the Knight KB5 — a grave concession. However, Black is entitled to despair. (Kmoch.)

32	N—B5	B x P
33	N—K7ch	K—R1
34	N—B6!	....

Forcing Black to exchange his powerful Queen Bishop.

34	....	B x N
35	Q x B	N—K1
36	P—Q7	Q—R2ch
37	K—R1	N—B2
38	R—KB1	K—N1
39	Q—B3!	Q—R1

If 39...P—B3; 40 B—B5, with a stranglehold on the white squares.

| 40 | Q x Q | N x Q |

| 41 | R—Q6 | K—B1 |
| 42 | R x QRP | K—K2 |

Black's lonely Knight now becomes the subject of the day.

43	R—QB6	P—B3
44	P—R4	P x P
45	R—R1	R—KB1
46	B—B5	R—Q1
47	R x RP	B—B1
48	R—K6ch	K x P

Or 48 . . . K—B2; 49 R—K8, R x R; 50 B—N6ch! and wins.

49	R—R7ch	N—B2
50	R—N6 dis ch	K—K1
51	R x N	B—Q3
52	R—KR7	Resigns

Do not be misled by the length of the following game, for almost every one of the eighty-one moves is a lesson.

"The classic minority attack is the main theme of this party, and interwoven in the magic pattern is a glorious Knight's tour and a very instructive Rook and Pawn ending." —*Chess Review*

No. 11

EVANS vs. OPSAHL
(U.S.A.)   (Norway)
Queen's Gambit Declined
Chess Olympic: Yugoslavia, 1950

	White	Black
1	P—Q4	N—KB3
2	P—QB3	P—K3
3	N—QB3	P—Q4

Transposing into a Queen's Gambit Declined.

| 4 | B—N5 | QN—Q2 |
| 5 | P—K3 | . . . . |

Avoiding the standard trap: 5 P x P, P x P; 6 N x P?, N x N!; 7 B x Q, B—N5ch; 8 Q—Q2, B x Qch; 9 K x B, K x B emerging a piece ahead.

5	B—K2
6 Q—B2	O—O
7 P x P	....

The exchange variation. 7 N—B3 is a satisfactory alternative. In either event White keeps the initiative.

7	P x P
8 N—B3	P—B3
9 B—Q3	R—K1
10 O—O	N—B1
11 QR—N1	....

Preparing the minority attack—all of which has been done thousands of times. Basically White's plan is to weaken the position of Black's Queen-side Pawn majority by the advance P—QN4—N5. White must create a weakness — a target to attack on the Queen flank; Black, on the other hand, must take vigorous countermeasures on the opposite wing.

11	N—K5
12 B x B	Q x B
13 P—QN4	....

The minority attack — White's two Queen-side Pawns are to be used as a battering ram against Black's three Pawns on the same wing.

| 13 .... | P—QR3 |

Temporarily forestalling P—N5.

| 14 P—QR4 | N x N |

14 ... P—KB4 is more active.

| 15 Q x N | B—N5 |
| 16 N—Q2 | .... |

After 15 N—K5, B—R4 the Knight will be driven back with loss of time by ... P—B3.

| 16 .... | Q—N4 |

Preparing the attack.

17 KR—B1	R—K3
18 P—N5	RP x P
19 P x P	....

The idea is to destroy the base of the Black Pawns.

| 19 .... | B—R6 |
| 20 P—N3 | QR—K1 |

Black cannot just shrug off the minority attack by 20 . . . P x P, since after 21 R x P he remains with an isolated Queen Pawn and a Queen Knight Pawn under fire.

| 21 P x P | P x P |

White has achieved his object: the Queen Bishop Pawn has become a target.

| 22 B—B1 | .... |

Easy does it! Not 22 R—N6, R x P!!; 27 P x R, Q x Pch; 28 K—R1, Q—B7 and wins, e.g., 29 B—B1, R—K7!; or 29 R—KN1, R—K8!; 30 R—N1, Q—N7 mate!

22	B x B
23 N x B	N—N3
24 R—N6	N—K2

As usual in this variation, Black's attack has backfired and he is saddled with a weak Pawn.

25 Q—N4	P—R4
26 R—N8	R x R
27 Q x Rch	K—R2
28 Q—B4	....

Queens must be exchanged so that the weak Queen Bishop Pawn can be exploited in the end game.

| 28 .... | Q x Q |

Weak. 28 . . . Q—N3 followed by . . . R—B3 should draw handily. Black should never exchange Queens unless his back is to the wall. Still, it is improper to say that White wins by force from this point on.

| 29 NP x Q | P—N3 |

Needlessly weakening the Pawn structure. 29 . . . R—N3ch is in order.

30 N—Q2	R—Q3
31 K—B1	K—N2
32 R—R1	....

There are more prospects on the open file.

| 32 .... | R—Q2 |

To prevent 33 R—7.

| 33 N—N3 | R—N2 |
| 34 N—B5 | R—N7 |

Finally getting the Rook to a good square. If Black attempts to hold on for dear life by 34 ... R—B2, then R—R8 followed by a King excursion to QN6 or a breakthrough with P—B3 and P—K4 is decisive.

35 R—R7	K—B3
36 R—R6	R—N8ch
37 K—N2	R—N7
38 R—R7	R—N8
39 R—B7	R—QR8

39 ... R—N7 would have made White's life much more miserable because the Bishop Pawn would remain pinned. The importance of this becomes apparent in the note to Black's forty-fifth move.

| 40 N—Q3 | .... |

40 N—Q7 ch immediately is more accurate.

| 40 .... | K—K3 |

Not 40 ... R—R7; 41 N—N4.

Curiously enough, White now discovers an amazing forced win based on a Knight's tour!

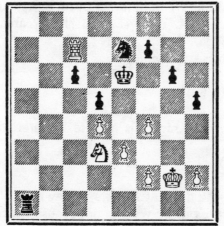

Diagram 176

41 N—B5ch   ....

The beginning of a bizarre circular maneuver resulting in the win of a Pawn.

41 ....   **K—B3**

Forced. Not 41 ... K—Q3 because of 42 R—Q7 mate!

42 N—Q7ch   **K—K3**

Again forced. On 42 ... K—N2 43 N—K5 wins a Pawn.

43 N—B8ch   **K—B3**

44 N—R7ch   **K—K3**

Black is unable to get off the merry-go-round. If 44 ... K—N2; 45 R x N, K x N; 46 R x Pch wins.

45 N—N5ch   ....

Thereby describing a circular tour of the board.

45 ....   **K—Q3**

The whole point of White's previous play (including the exclusion of Black's Rook from the seventh rank) becomes clear in the following variation: 45 ... K—B3; 46 P—B3!! and Black is helpless against the P—K4—5 advance.

46 R—N7   ....

Winning a Pawn by force.

46 ....   **P—B3**

It is too bad that all the thoughts which run through a tournament player's mind never appear in the notes. Another pretty point to White's combination is brought out by the defense with 46 ... P—B4, e.g., 47 N—R7! (threatening N—B8), K—K3; 48 N—B8ch, K—B2; 49 N x P!, K x N; 50 R x N winning an important Pawn.

47 N—R7   **K—K3**

Not ... P—B4?; 48 N—B8.

48 N—B8ch   ....

Returning with the Knight, as it were, counterclockwise.

48 ....   **K—B2**

49 N x P   **K x N**

50 R x N   ....

Now we enter the difficult Rook and Pawn ending. White is a Pawn ahead, true, but he wins only because Black's insecure, neurotic, and isolated Queen Bishop Pawn is indefensible.

50	....	K—B4
51	R—QB7	R—QB8
52	R—B8	K—N3
53	K—N3	R—B7
54	P—R4	K—B4
55	R—KR8	K—N3
56	P—B5ch	....

Dissolving the doubled Pawn and establishing a passed King Rook Pawn. The basic rule for end games of this sort is to create an outside passed Pawn.

56	....	K x P

After 56 ... K—N2; 57 R x P, the Rook is trapped but it cannot be attacked; yet there is no need for White to enter such a risky variation. After 56 ... K—N2; 57 R—QB8 followed by P—B3, K—B4, and eventually P—K4 is decisive. In the meantime, Black is in virtual Zugzwang.

57	R x Pch	K—N3
58	R—R8	....

The first stage of the ending is over. The rest is still tough.

58	....	K—B4
59	R—KN8	....

Cutting off the King.

59	....	R—B8

Threatening 60 ... R—N8ch.

60	K—N2	R—QR8
61	P—R5	R—R2
62	R—N3	....

A general principle: Rooks belong behind passed Pawns.

62	....	R—R2
63	R—R3	K—N4
64	K—B3!	.....

White cannot retain his extra Pawn, but he continually threatens to transpose into a winning King and Pawn ending — the "sword of Damocles" motif, whereby the Pawn is used to make inroads.

64 ....   **R—R3**

If 64 ... R x P; 65 R x R, K x R; 66 K—B4 and wins. Eventually Black is forced to enter this variation.

65 R—R1   **K—B4**

Trying to keep the King out.

66 K—N3   **K—N4**

Or 66 ... R—R1; 67 P—R6 and sooner or later Black will be forced to accept the Pawn under unfavorable circumstances.

67 R—R4   **K—B4**
68 R—B4ch   **K—N4**
69 R—N4ch   **K—B4**

Again if 69 ... K x P; 70 R—R4ch, K—N4; 71 R x R, K x R; 72 K—N4, K—N3; 73 K—B4 and White wins.

70 K—R4   **R—R1**
71 R—N7   **R—R1**

Trying to get behind the passed Pawn. Where it stands now, the Rook is doomed to passivity.

72 P—R6   **R—R8**
73 R—N3   **R—R8ch**
74 R—R3   **R—KN8**
75 R—B3ch!   **....**

And not the hasty 75 P—R7?, R—N5ch; 76 K—R5, R—N4ch with a draw by perpetual check.

75 ....   **K—N3**
76 R—N3ch   **R x R**
77 K x R   **K x P**
78 K—N4   **K—N3**
79 K—B4   **....**

White wins because he has the opposition. Black does not wish to, but he *must* move.

79 ....   **K—N2**

On 79 ... P—B4; 80 K—K5 followed by K—Q6 wins outright.

80 K—B5   **K—B2**
81 P—B3!   **Resigns**

Diagram 177

White has the opposition and must make a decisive inroad via N6 or K6; for example, 81 ... K—K2; 82 K—N6, K—K3; 83 P—B4, P—B4 (if 83 ... K—K2; 84 P—B5 wins the Bishop Pawn); 84 K—N5 winning the Bishop Pawn and the game.

The ending is a classic-illustration of the importance of the opposition.

No. 12

NAJDORF vs. KRAMER
Catalan System
Amsterdam, 1950

White	Black
1 P—Q4	N—KB3
2 P—QB4	P—K3
3 P—KN3	....

Slow development. As in Game No. 8, we see the tendency to delay the immediate fight.

3	P—Q4
4 B—N2	P x P

Black's continuation is good enough for equality. Another solid variation is 3 ... P—QB3 followed by ... P—QN3 and B—N2 with an eventual break with ... P—QB4. The text has

the drawback of allowing White to unleash the full fury of
his King Bishop.

| 5 N—KB3 | QN—Q2 |

More energetic is 5 . . . P—B4; 6 Q—R4ch, B—Q2; 7 Q x
BP, N—B3; 8 P x P, Q—R4ch.

| 6 QN—Q2 | . . . . |

Q—R4 is more usual.

6	N—N3
7 O—O	P—B4
8 N x P	N x N
9 Q—R4ch	B—Q2
10 Q x N	Q—N3

The position is critical. Black seems to have a satisfactory
game; but he cannot prevent N—K5 in the long run and his
Queen Bishop is worth less than White's King Bishop.

11 P—N3	B—N4
12 Q—B2	P x P
13 B—N2	P—Q6

The Pawn cannot be held.

| 14 P x P | . . . . |

White's pieces are better placed and this compensates for
his bad Pawn structure.

| 14 . . . . | B—K2 |

Better is 14 . . . B—B3! to render N—K5 ineffectual. He need
not fear 15 B x N.

| 15 N—K5 | . . . . |

White's advantage is small but now undeniable. His Bishops
both bear down on important diagonals and Black has some
difficulty in protecting his Queen Knight Pawn — it is uneconomical to do so with a Queen.

| 15 . . . . | O—O |
| 16 QR—B1 | KR—Q1 |

A "natural" move. It is difficult to suggest better, Black might
try 16 . . . B—R3 followed by . . . Q—Q1 in order to contest the
QB file by . . . R—QB1.

17 KR—K1	N—Q4

Threatening 18 ... N—N5.

18 Q—K2	B—KB3

18 ... B—K1 prevents White's ensuing maneuver which forces a weakening in Black's King-side armor.

19 Q—R5!	B—K1
20 B—K4!	P—N3

... P—KR3 is a less serious weakening move. White prepares his attack quickly — and from almost nothing. That is what is so amazing!

21 .Q—K2	....

Intending 22 N—N4, B—Q5; 23 R—B4! Where did Black go wrong?

21	QR—B1
22 N—N4	B—Q5

Diagram 178

After 22 ... B x B; 23 Q x B Black is too weak on the dark squares.

Now, however, Najdorf wins by force!

23 R x R	R x R
24 B x N!	P x B
25⁻ N—R6ch	K—B1

On 25 ... K—N2; 26 Q—N4, B x B; 27 Q x R wins the exchange. Or if 25 ...K –R1; 26 Q–K7, K–N2 transposing into the actual game.

26	Q–K7ch	K–N2
27	R–K6!!	....

The finest move in the game.

| 27 | .... | B x B |

What makes Najdorf's combination so pretty are the various ways that Black can decline: (1) 27 ... Q x R; 28 B x Bch, K x N; 29 Q–R4 mate; (2) 27 ... R–B8ch; 28 K–N2!, B x B; 29 R x Q, P x R; 30 Q x B and White should win quickly; (3) 27 ... R–B3; 28 N–B5ch!, P x N; 29 Q–N5ch, K–B1; 30 Q–R6ch, K–N1; 31 R x B mate.

The text move is Black's best chance and still leaves quite a bit of fight.

28	R x Q	P x R
29	N–N4	....

Not 29 Q x P?, R–B8ch followed by 30 ... K x N.

| 29 | .... | B–QB3 |

Black has a Rook and a Bishop for a Queen – often a fair match since they total 8 to the Queen's 10 units in the Table of Relative Values. Here, however, "all other things are not equal" because White has a Queen *and* Knight against a Rook and *two* Bishops; the presence of the Knight radically changes the dynamics of the position since in combination with the Queen and Pawns it is sufficient to produce a mating attack.

| 30 | N–K5 | .... |

30 P–KR4 seems more logical.

30	....	B x N
31	Q x Bch	K–N1
32	P–QR4	R–K1
33	Q–Q4	P–QN4
34	P–R5!	....

The ending is hopeless for Black. White's objective is to keep as many Pawns on the board as possible and make inroads with his Queen on the black squares.

34	....	R–K3
35	P–B4	P–R3

A needless weakening move. Black should try to keep his King position intact. To guard against the advance of White's King-side Pawns (P–KN4–B5) he should try 35 . . . P–B4 which has the drawback of exposing the King and the merit of holding the position – for a while.

36 K–B2   K–R2

Still 36 . . . P–B4 is called for.

37 P–KN4   P–B3

38 Q–N6

Black exceeded the time limit – forfeit.

In tournament chess the usual time limit is forty moves in two hours. If either player fails to make the required number of moves within the allotted time, he automatically forfeits the game.

In this position Black is lost no matter what he does. The immediate threat is 39 P–B5, P x P; 40 P x P, R–Q3; 41 P–R6!, P x P; 42 Q–B7ch winning at least a piece. Black's sole defensive try is 38 . . . P–B4, after which 39 Q–B7ch, K–N1; 40 P x P, P x P; 41 Q–B8ch, K–B2; 42 Q–KR8! should quickly decide the issue, although Black can still hold on a while with 42 . . . R–B3. In such an event, 43 K–K3 followed by 44 K–Q4 puts an end to his struggles.

Here the author of *White To Play And Win* goes all out to prove it. But he soon discovers that Black's position is slaughter-repellent.

No. 13

ADAMS vs. EVANS
Log Cabin C.C.   Marshall C.C.
Sicilian Defense
New York Metropolitan League Match, 1951

White   Black

1 P–K4   . . . .

It is interesting to note that Adams invariably opens in this manner. On the other hand Gruenfeld, when asked why he avoided 1 P–K4, replied, "I never make a mistake in the opening!"

1 . . . .   P–QB4

I played the Sicilian Defense on the spur of the moment, not wishing to counter my opponent's pet Vienna Opening: 1 ...P—K4; 2 N—QB3.

2	N—KB3	P—Q3
3	P—Q4	P x P
4	N x P	N—KB3
5	N—QB3	P—QR3

A temporizing move which prepares ...P—QN4, B—N2, Q —B2, and R—B1 with pressure on the Queen's flank. The more usual move is 5...P—KN3, but at the last minute I recalled a game at the Pan-American Tournament, 1945, in which Adams busted Reshevsky in the opening with 6 P—KR3.

| 6 | P—KR3 | .... |

Preparing the ultra-aggressive P—KN4. 6 P—KN3, however, is stronger.

| 6 | .... | P—QN4 |
| 7 | P—KN4 | B—N2 |

Not 7...P—N5; 8 N—Q5!, N x P?; 9B—N2.

| 8 | B—N2 | P—K3 |

Finally threatening 9...P—N5.

| 9 | Q—K2 | .... |

More consistent is 9 P—N5, with attack.

| 9 | .... | Q—B2 |

Even sharper is 9...P—N5; 10 N—Q1, P—Q4!
White should now play 10 P—N5...

| 10 | P—B4 | .... |

...which he neglects to do. This move weakens, not strengthens, his center.

| 10 | .... | P—N5 |
| 11 | N—Q1 | P—Q4! |

An attack on one of the wings is usually best met by a counteraction in the center of the board.

| 12 | P—K5 | .... |

12 P x P, B x P! with a splendid game.

| 12 | .... | N—K5! |

Energetic measures are called for. In order to prevent ...
N—N6 White must part with his precious Bishop.

13	B x N	P x B
14	B—K3	....

The weakness on the white squares precludes the win of the
King Pawn, e.g., 14 N—B2, P—K6! winning a piece because of
the attack on the Rook.

14	....	N—Q2

The secret of a successful counterattack is development.
During the lull, Black takes time out to bring his Queen Knight
into play.

15	N—B2	....

15 P—KR4 would have prevented Black's next move, but
the advanced King-side Pawns would sooner or later prove to
be White's undoing.

15	....	P—N4!

Crippling the center and securing maximum activity for the
pieces. The main threat is 16 ... B—N2 followed by the win
of White's King Pawn.

16	P—B5	....

There is nothing better. If 16 O—O—O, P x P; 17 B x P,
P—K6 wins.

16	....	Q x KP
17	P x P	P x P
18	P—KR4!	....

The open King Rook file is White's best chance for counterplay.

18	....	B—B4
19	O—O—O	N—N3!

On 19 ... P x P; 20 R x P, White threatens either 21 R—R5
or R—R6 and Black's King remains exposed in the center.

20	P x P	N—Q4
21	R—R6	....

How does Black best meet the threat of 22 R x Pch?

21	....	O—O!

Diagram 179

Defense and attack! Black now hatches his own threat: 22 ... N x B; 23 Q x N, R—B6.

22 R x KP   . . . .

Virtually forced.

22 . . . .   **Resigns**

Q x R!

Black obtains a Rook and two Bishops for his Queen, and he still retains a winning attack: 23 N x Q, B x Bch; 24 K—N1, R x N followed by 25 ... R—QB1. Incidentally, three minor pieces are nearly always as strong as a Queen — and Rook and two minor pieces are usually much stronger, other things being equal.

No. 14

EUWE   vs.   EVANS
(Holland)   (U.S.A.)
Queen's Indian Defense
Wertheim Memorial Tournament, 1951

	White	Black
1	P—Q4	N—KB3
2	P—QB4	P—K3
3	N—KB3	P—QN3

The move typifies the Queen's Indian Defense, in Russia called the West Indian Defense. The name is derived from the fact that the game played in India does not have the initial double Pawn move, so that the slower type of development which is so characteristic of this opening is seen there much more often.

4	P—KN3	B—N2
5	B—N2	B—K2
6	O—O	O—O

If 6 ... P—B4; 7 P—Q5!, P x P; 8 N—R4! gives White the advantage.

| 7 | N—B3 | N—K5 |

In this game Black must prevent White from playing P—K4 at all costs; the fight, therefore, revolves around Black's K5 square.

| 8 | Q—B2 | N x N |
| 9 | Q x N | .... |

Not 9 N—N5?, N x Pch! and wins.

9	....	P—KB4
10	N—K1	B x B
11	N x B	....

All book. The Knight will soon obtain a strong post at KB4.

| 11 | .... | B—B3 |

Since I was going all out to beat the former World Champion, I chose this aggressive but theoretically inferior line. An alternative is 11 ... Q—K1; 12 Q—B2 (to force P—K4), N—B3; 13 B—K3, P—K4.

| 12 | B—K3 | .... |

Black was threatening 12 ... P—B4 followed by ... N—B3 with pressure.

12	....	P—Q3
13	Q—B2	Q—B1
14	N—B4	P—B3

White was threatening 15 P—Q5, P—K4; 16 N—K6. In such positions Anderssen used to say, "Once you get a Knight firmly planted on K6 you can go to sleep. Your game will then play itself!"

15 Q—N3   ....

Angling for P—Q5, which could not be played immediately because of ... BP x P!

15 ....   P—KN4!?

A risky move which must be played to prevent P—Q5.

16 N—R5!   ....

Euwe accepts the challenge, scorning the safer 16 N—Q3.

16 ....   B—K2
17 P—B5!   P—Q4

I consumed a half hour on this move. If 17 ... NP x P; 18 P x P, P—Q4 (not ... P x P; 19 Q—B3 with a bind.) The text, however, involves the sacrifice of the Queen Knight Pawn.

18 P x P   P x P
19 P—B3   ....

Getting cold feet at the last moment. White should play 19 Q x P, Q—K1; 20 P—KN4, P x P; 21 N—N3 with a difficult game for both sides.

19 ....   N—Q2

Now all Black's pieces are ideally posted and he maintains the option of a break by ... P—QB4.

20 P—N4   ....

He is too much concerned with the Knight which is out on a limb. 20 QR—B1 must be played instead.

20 ....   Q—R3!
21 Q—B2   Q—B5!

Forcing the exchange of Queens at the expense of doubled Pawns — which in this case are in Black's favor since he can control the open Queen side lines. White is at a loss for a good reply.

22 Q x Q   ....

If 22 Q—Q2, R x P; or on 22 KR—B1, Q x Q; 23 R x Q, P—B4 with advantage.

22 ....   P x Q
23 P—B4   ....

Diagram 180

Black now forces a won end game, but it is difficult to suggest better.

23	....	P x NP
24	P x P	R x Rch
25	K x R	P—N4

The general advance of the Queen-side Pawns produces a decisive passed Pawn on that wing. White's Rook is tied down and his Knight is out of play.

| 26 | K—N2 | N—N3 |
| 27 | K—N3 | P—N5 |

There is no time to stop and defend.

| 28 | K x P | P—N6 |
| 29 | P—Q5 | .... |

An ingenious desperation attempt. After the game Euwe suggested 29 P—R3, but then 29 ... P—B6 followed by ... N—B5 decides the issue.

29	....	N x P
30	B—Q4	P x P
31	N—B6ch	B x N
32	P x B	N—N5

Threatening ... N—B7.

| 33 | K—B4 | K—B2! |

Safety first! Not 33...N—B7; 34 R—N1ch, K—B1; 35 B—
B5ch, K—B2; 36 K—K5, R—N1; 37 R x R, K x R; 38 K x P!!,
P—R8=Q; 39 P—B7 ch and wins! By losing a tempo, Black
now wins the game!

34 B—K5   ....

Now 34 R—KN1 is met by...R—KN1; 35 R—QR1, N—B7
picking up a piece.

34	....	N—B7
35	R—Q1	P—R8=Q
36	R—Q7ch	K—K1
37	R—K7ch	

Or 37 P—B7 ch, K x R and the Rook on the first rank prevents
the Pawn from queening — an optical illusion!

37	....	K—B1
38	R x P	Q—KB8ch
39	K—N3	Q—B4
	Resigns	

White is left with a few more checks, but eventually he must
bow to Black's material superiority.

No. 15

EVANS vs. SANTASIERE
Nimzo-Indian Defense
United States Championship, 1951

	White	Black
1	P—Q4	N—KB3
2	P—QB4	P—K3
3	N—QB3	B—N5
4	P—K3	P—QN3
5	N—K2	N—K5!?

An innovation which this game refutes. More customary is
5...B—N2 or even...B—R3!? as introduced by Bronstein
in his match against Botvinnik, 1951.

| 6 | P—B3 | N x N |
| 7 | P x N | B—K2 |

We can now appraise the net result of Black's opening play: he has succeeded in doubling White's Queen Bishop Pawns, but at the cost of time, center, and development.

8	P—K4	N—B3
9	N—N3	B—R3
10	B—Q3	N—R4
11	Q—K2	....

Just in time!

11	....	O—O
12	O—O	P—Q4

More consistent is 12 ... P—B4; 13 B—K3, QR—B1, though White remains with the better game after QR—B1. Or White may elect to play 13 P—Q5 (after 12 ... P—B4).

13	BP x P	B x B
14	Q x B	P x P
15	N—B5!	....

An important in-between move. White, by threatening to win a Pawn with P x P, lures the Black Rook to K1. It is essential to do so since Black will not later have ... P—KB4 at his disposal as a defensive move.

15	....	R—K1

Best. If 15 ... Px P; 16 P x P and the Queen has KN3 at its disposal.

16	P—K5	P—B4
17	P—KB4	....

Threatening 18 Q—N3, P—N3; 19 N—R6ch, K—B1; 20 P—B5 with an irresistible onslaught.

17	....	Q—Q2
18	R—B3	B—B1

... N—B5 immediately is the best chance, though hardly sufficient.

19	R—R3	P—N3

White was threatening 20 N—K7 ch followed by Q x P mate.

20	N—K3	P x P
21	P x P	QR—B1

22	P—B5	N—B5
23	N—N4	B—N2

Forced, to prevent N—B6ch. Now, however, White has a forced win. Black, it is true, has made no outright errors in his defense; but his hopeless position may be traced back directly to the opening: 5...N—K5!? The move in itself was ill-conceived, and it forced Black to continue with a series of time-losing maneuvers. White, in the interim, consolidated his center and prepared his attack. Before Santasiere could think of the Italian word for check, he was overwhelmed with a host of threats.

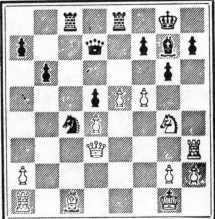

Diagram 181

24	R x P!!	. . . .

Quite wrong was a published criticism of this move on the grounds that 24 N—R6ch also wins with less risk.

24	. . . .	K x R

Working on the principle that the best way to refute a sacrifice is to accept it. There is, however, no satisfactory way to decline the Grecian gift; for if 24 . . . Q x P; 25 Q—R3, threatening 26 R x Bch, wins.

25	Q—R3ch	K—N1
26	P—B6!	. . . .

The point. Not 25 P x P because of . . . Q—K3. Now Black

cannot meet the double threat of either 27 P x B or N—R6ch.

| 26 | .... | Q x N |

Desperation. The relatively best defense is 26 ... Q—R5!, though after 27 P x B, Q—Q8ch; 28 K—B2, Q x Pch; 29 B—K3, Q—N7ch; 30 K—N3, P—B4!; 31 Q—R8ch, K—B2; 32 Q—R7! White should still win.

| 27 | Q x Q | B x P |

Giving up a second piece. After 27 ... B—B1; 28 P—KR4 followed by P—R5 quickly decides the outcome.

| 28 | P x B | R—K8ch |
| 29 | K—B2 | QR—K1 |

Black has a Rook for a Queen and a few spite checks — hardly sufficient.

30	P—KR4	R(1)—K5
31	Q—N5	R(5)—K7ch
32	K—N3	N—Q3

Threatening 33 ... N—K5ch.

33	K—R2	N—K5
34	Q x P	N x P
35	Q—Q8ch	N—K1
36	B—N2	R x R

"Resigns" was an attractive alternative.

37	B x R	P—B3
38	P—Q5	R—K5
39	P—Q6	....

Nimzovitch described the march of the Pawn to the queening square as the "lust to expand."

39	....	R x Pch
40	K—N3	R—K5
41	P—Q7	Resigns

No. 16
PRINS AND EVANS vs. RESHEVSKY AND HOROWITZ
Sicilian Defense

Consultation Game, New York, 1951

White	Black
1 P—K4	P—QB4
2 N—KB3	P—Q3
3 P—Q4	P x P
4 N x P	N—KB3
5 P—KB3	....

Theoretisches Spiel! This move has been known for a long time but Prins had some prepared analysis which we decided to give the acid test.

5 ....   P—K4

In order to prevent 6 P—QB4, Black must immediately break in the center; but not 5...P—Q4; 6 P—K5 and P—K6. The text is virtually forced.

6 N—N3   ....

The "new" move. The older 6 N—QN5, P—Q4!; 7 P x P, B—QB4! is unpleasant, while 6 B—N5ch yields no advantage.

| 6 .... | P—Q4 |
| 7 B—N5 | B—K3 |

7...P—Q5; 8 P—B3 is in White's favor.

| 8 P x P | Q x P |
| 9 N—B3 | B—N5 |

9...Q x Qch is no better.

10 B—Q2!   Q—Q1!

An improvement over 10...B x N; 11 B x B, N—B3; 12 B—Q3 with advantage, as in Prins-Pirc, Bad Pyrmont, 1951. Of course not 10...Q—Q2; 11 N—N5!

11 B—N5ch   ....

11 N—N5, N—B3; 12 B x B, N x B; 13 N—Q6ch, K—K2; 14 N x NP, Q—N3 with a dangerous attack.

11 ....   N—B3

11...QN—Q2 is safer but less forceful. The text eventually makes White part with the two Bishops.

| 12 | Q—K2 | O—O |
| 13 | B x N | .... |

More or less forced, since if 13 O—O—O, B x N; 14 RP x B, N—Q5; 15 Q x P, P—R3! with vigorous counterplay, White's extra Pawn counting for nothing.

| 13 | .... | P x B |
| 14 | O—O—O | .... |

Obviously not 14 Q x P, B x N; 15 RP x B, R—K1 winning the Queen. We spent some time considering 14 O—O but finally discarded it because Black has too many tactical possibilities on the QR2—KN8 diagonal.

| 14 | .... | Q—B2 |
| 15 | N—K4 | .... |

On 15 N—R4 follows P—B4! This is the critical position where White must prove that Black's weak Pawn structure offsets Black's attack and the two Bishops.

Diagram 182

| 15 | .... | P—QR4? |

A fighting move which leads to sharp play; however, better is 15 ... B x Bch; 16 N(3) or N(4) x B (weaker is 16 R x B, N x N; 17 Q x N, P—QB4) with approximately equal play. On 15 ... N—Q4 comes N(3)—B5.

| 16 | N x Nch | P x N |
| 17 | Q—B2 | .... |

17 B—R6 is more accurate.

17	KR—Q1

17 ... K—R1 immediately saves a tempo. On 17 ... P—R5; 18 B—R6 wins, while after 17 ... B x Bch; 18 N x B, Black is very weak on the dark-colored squares.

18 B—R6	K—R1
19 N—B5	....

We were too short of time to delve deeply into the consequencies of 19 P—B4, P—R5; 20 P x P, Q x P; 21 N—Q4, P—R6!

19	R—KN1

19 ... B x N; 20 Q x B leads to opposite-colored Bishops but White has a bind. And if 19 ... B x P; 20 Q—R4, Q—K2; 21 N—K4 wins, e.g., 21 ... B—R6; 22 N x P (Threatening 23 B—N7ch), Q—N5; 23 B—N7ch, K x B; 24 N—R5ch forces mate.

R—N3	20 Q—R4

20 ... Q—K2 is slightly stronger.

21 N x B	P x N
22 R—Q3	B—K2

If 22 ... R—Q1; 23 R x Rch, Q x R; 24 R—Q1, Q—K2; 25 P—N3 followed by pressure against Black's weak Queenside Pawns.

23 KR—Q1	P—KB4
24 Q—R5	R—Q1
25 R x Rch	B x R
26 P—KN4!	....

Threatening 27 P x P, P x P; 28 Q x P! (28 ... R x B; 29 Q—B8 mate).

26	P—B5

Relatively better is 26 ... B—B3; 27 P x P, P x P; 28 B—K3 with an overwhelming position. White was in mild, Black in severe, time pressure.

27 B—B8	B—B3
28 B—B5	....

Not 28 B—Q6, Q—N3 with counterchances. The threat is now 29 R—Q6.

28 ....   P—K5

Whistling in the dark. If instead 28...K—N2; 29 P—KR4 wins.

29 P x P   P—B6

Prins muttered, "We refuse to be impressed!"

30 B—Q6   Q—N3

On 30...Q—KN2; 31 B—K5! simplifies to White's advantage.

31 B—K5   Q—K6ch
32 K—N1   ....

Diagram 183

32 ....   Q x P

After the game many analysts claimed that 32...K—N2 "would have drawn the game." Although it is relatively better, it can be refuted in the following manner: 32...K—N2; 33 B x Bch!, K x B (if 33...R x B; 34 Q—K5, K—B2; 35 P—N5 spells finis); 34 P—K5ch, Q x P (if 34...K—N2; 35 P—QR3, P—B7; 36 K—R2, threatening R—Q7ch wins); 35 P—N5ch, Q x P; 36 Q x Pch, K—N2; 37 Q x P and White wins with ease.

33 B x Bch   R x B
34 Q—K8ch   K—N2

"Are you sure this is the right position?" queried Prins, unable to believe his eyes.

35 R—Q7ch   **Resigns**
For if 35 . . . K—R3; 36 Q—R5 mate.

APPENDIX
THE OFFICIAL LAWS OF CHESS

MODERNIZED VERSION USED BY
UNITED STATES CHESS FEDERATION

I. Definition and Object

I. Chess is played by two persons on a square board called the Chessboard and divided into 64 squares colored light and dark alternately. Each person shall play with a series of sixteen men, one series to be light-colored and called White, and the other series to be dark-colored and called Black.

II. The object of the play is to checkmate the opponent's King and the player who checkmates thereby wins the game.

2. The Chessboard

I. The Chessboard shall be so placed between the two persons that the nearer corner square at their respective right hands shall be light-colored.

II. The Queen shall be placed on its own color.

3. Movement of the Men in General

I. The move of a man shall be to an unoccupied square or to a square occupied by an opposing man.

II. The move of a man shall not cause such man to pass over any occupied square, except in the case of the move of the Knight.

III. A legal move of a man to a square occupied by an opposing man requires the removal of that opposing man by the player from the Chessboard.

IV. The first move in a game shall be made with a White man.

V. The persons shall play alternately, one move at a time.

VI. The choice of playing the first game with the White men or the Black men shall be determined by lot, or by agreement, and in a match of two or more games the two persons shall play with the two series alternately, irrespective of the results of the games, but games annulled shall not be reckoned in applying this rule.

VII. A capture is optional with the player unless it is the only possible move.

VIII. In castling, the King shall first be moved and then the Rook; or both pieces may be moved simultaneously.

IX. A legal move cannot be retracted.

4. Annulled Games

I. If in the course of or *immediately after* a game it be proved that the initial position of the men on the board was incorrect, or the Chessboard wrongly placed initially, the game shall be annulled.

II. If in the course of a game the number or position of the men be altered illegally, the position immediately before the alteration occurred must be reinstated and the game resumed therefrom.

III. If this position cannot be ascertained the game shall be annulled and there shall be a replay.

5. Completion of Move

I. A move is complete:

(a) In moving a man from one square to another, when the player has quitted the man.

(b) In capturing, when the captured man has been removed from the board and the player has quitted the man making the capture.

(c) In castling, when the player has quitted the Rook.

(d) In promoting a Pawn, when the player has replaced the Pawn by the selected piece and quitted the latter.

6. Adjustment of the Men

I. The player may adjust one or more of his men on their respective squares after giving previous notice of his intention to do so. (Note: It is customary to use the expression "I adjust.")

II. The player shall not adjust the opponent's men, or the opponent the player's men. The opponent, however, shall adjust the position of his men on the board if requested by the player.

7. Touching Men

If the player touch:

(a) One of his own men he must move it;

(b) One of the opponent's men he must take it;

(c) One of his own men and one of the opponent's men, he must take the latter with the former, if such capture be a legal move. If not, the opponent may require either that the player shall move his man touched, or take the opponent's man touched with any one of the men at the player's option with which the capture can be effected legally.

(If none of the moves indicated in a, b, or c can be made legally, no penalty can be exacted.)

If the player touch:

(d) Several of his own men, the opponent has the right to name which of these men the player shall move. If none of these men can be moved legally, no penalty can be exacted.

If the player touch:

(e) Several of the opponent's men, the opponent has the right to name which man shall be taken. If none of these men can be taken, no penalty can be exacted.

A legal move cannot be retracted.

8. Drawn Games

The game is drawn:

(a) When the player cannot make a legal move and the King is not in check. The King is then said to be stalemated.

(b) If the player prove he can subject the opponent's King to an endless series of checks (perpetual check).

(c) By recurrence of position when the same position occurs three times in the game, and the same person is player on each occasion, and if such player claim the draw before the position is altered by further play; otherwise no claim can be sustained.

(d) By mutual agreement, but only after 30 moves have been made with the Black men.

(e) If the player prove that 50 moves have been made on each side without checkmate having been given and without any man having been captured or Pawn moved. Either the player or the opponent may at any period of the game demand that the other shall checkmate him in 50 moves (subject to the conditions attached in e). If checkmate is not given in 50 moves, the game shall be declared drawn. Nevertheless, the count of 50 moves shall begin again after each capture of any man and after each movement of a Pawn. Exception shall be made for certain positions where theoretically more than 50 moves are necessary to force a checkmate, and in this case a number of moves double the number established in theory as being necessary for this object shall be allowed in lieu of the 50. The draw must be claimed by either the player or the opponent immediately the stipulated number of moves in the particular case is completed, and not at any later period.

9. **Illegal Moves**

If a player make an illegal move and the opponent draw attention to the fact before touching any of his own men, the illegal move must be retracted, and the game shall be continued as follows:

(a) When a capture has not been made, the player shall make a legal move with the man he moved illegally, but if no such legal move can be made no penalty can be exacted.

(b) If a capture has been made, the player must either take the opponent's man by a legal move, or make a legal move with his own man touched at the option of the opponent, but if no such legal move can be made no penalty can be exacted.

(c) If in the course of a game it is proved that an illegal move has been made and not retracted, the position existing immediately before the illegal move was made shall be reinstated and the game shall be continued from that position. If the position cannot be reinstated, the game shall be annulled.

10. Penalties

I. The opponent can exact a penalty for an infraction of these laws only if he has not touched one of his own men after the infraction occurred.

II. Castling cannot be exacted as a penalty move.

III. If the opponent names as penalty a move which is illegal, his right to exact a penalty for the illegality committed by the player shall be abrogated.

IV. Before enforcing any penalty the position which existed before the illegality occurred shall be reinstated.

11. Games Forfeited

The game shall be declared forfeited by the player or the opponent:

(a) Who wilfully upsets the board or disarranges the men;

(b) Who refuses to comply with a legal requirement under the laws;

(c) Who in the course of the game refuses to obey the rules and conform to the arrangements made for the conduct of the game.

Note: Except when unavoidably prevented, the competitors in a tournament shall conform to the directions of the official in charge.

ANNEXE
Conduct of Player and Opponent

I. Written or printed notes (except the record of moves made), dealing with or having any bearing on a game in progress shall not be referred to or utilized by the player or his opponent, and neither of them shall have recourse to any extraneous advice or information.

II. No analysis of games shall be allowed in the tournament rooms.

III. Neither player nor opponent shall make any comments on any of the moves in the game in progress between them.

IV. Neither player nor opponent shall touch or point to any square on the board for the purpose of facilitating reckoning possible moves.

V. A move shall be made by transferring the man touched directly towards the square to be occupied, and the man must be quitted immediately after it has been placed on that square.

In promoting a Pawn the player shall immediately remove the Pawn from the board and place the substituted piece on the vacated square.

VI. No comments of any kind or suggestions as to drawing or abandoning the game shall be added to a sealed move.

VII. Neither player nor opponent shall in any way whatsoever distract the attention of, or cause annoyance to, the other.

MELVIN POWERS SELF-IMPROVEMENT LIBRARY

ASTROLOGY
____ ASTROLOGY: HOW TO CHART YOUR HOROSCOPE *Max Heindel*   5.00
____ ASTROLOGY AND SEXUAL ANALYSIS *Morris C. Goodman*   5.00
____ ASTROLOGY AND YOU *Carroll Righter*   5.00
____ ASTROLOGY MADE EASY *Astarte*   5.00
____ ASTROLOGY, ROMANCE, YOU AND THE STARS *Anthony Norvell*   5.00
____ MY WORLD OF ASTROLOGY *Sydney Omarr*   7.00
____ THOUGHT DIAL *Sydney Omarr*   7.00
____ WHAT THE STARS REVEAL ABOUT THE MEN IN YOUR LIFE *Thelma White*   3.00

BRIDGE
____ BRIDGE BIDDING MADE EASY *Edwin B. Kantar*   10.00
____ BRIDGE CONVENTIONS *Edwin B. Kantar*   7.00
____ COMPETITIVE BIDDING IN MODERN BRIDGE *Edgar Kaplan*   7.00
____ DEFENSIVE BRIDGE PLAY COMPLETE *Edwin B. Kantar*   15.00
____ GAMESMAN BRIDGE—PLAY BETTER WITH KANTAR *Edwin B. Kantar*   5.00
____ HOW TO IMPROVE YOUR BRIDGE *Alfred Sheinwold*   7.00
____ IMPROVING YOUR BIDDING SKILLS *Edwin B. Kantar*   7.00
____ INTRODUCTION TO DECLARER'S PLAY *Edwin B. Kantar*   7.00
____ INTRODUCTION TO DEFENDER'S PLAY *Edwin B. Kantar*   7.00
____ KANTAR FOR THE DEFENSE *Edwin B. Kantar*   7.00
____ KANTAR FOR THE DEFENSE VOLUME 2 *Edwin B. Kantar*   7.00
____ TEST YOUR BRIDGE PLAY *Edwin B. Kantar*   5.00
____ VOLUME 2—TEST YOUR BRIDGE PLAY *Edwin B. Kantar*   7.00
____ WINNING DECLARER PLAY *Dorothy Hayden Truscott*   7.00

BUSINESS, STUDY & REFERENCE
____ BRAINSTORMING *Charles Clark*   7.00
____ CONVERSATION MADE EASY *Elliot Russell*   4.00
____ EXAM SECRET *Dennis B. Jackson*   3.00
____ FIX-IT BOOK *Arthur Symons*   2.00
____ HOW TO DEVELOP A BETTER SPEAKING VOICE *M. Hellier*   4.00
____ HOW TO SAVE 50% ON GAS & CAR EXPENSES *Ken Stansbie*   5.00
____ HOW TO SELF-PUBLISH YOUR BOOK & MAKE IT A BEST SELLER *Melvin Powers*   10.00
____ INCREASE YOUR LEARNING POWER *Geoffrey A. Dudley*   3.00
____ PRACTICAL GUIDE TO BETTER CONCENTRATION *Melvin Powers*   5.00
____ PRACTICAL GUIDE TO PUBLIC SPEAKING *Maurice Forley*   5.00
____ 7 DAYS TO FASTER READING *William S. Schaill*   5.00
____ SONGWRITERS' RHYMING DICTIONARY *Jane Shaw Whitfield*   7.00
____ SPELLING MADE EASY *Lester D. Basch & Dr. Milton Finkelstein*   3.00
____ STUDENT'S GUIDE TO BETTER GRADES *J. A. Rickard*   3.00
____ TEST YOURSELF—FIND YOUR HIDDEN TALENT *Jack Shafer*   3.00
____ YOUR WILL & WHAT TO DO ABOUT IT *Attorney Samuel G. Kling*   5.00

CALLIGRAPHY
____ ADVANCED CALLIGRAPHY *Katherine Jeffares*   7.00
____ CALLIGRAPHER'S REFERENCE BOOK *Anne Leptich & Jacque Evans*   7.00
____ CALLIGRAPHY—THE ART OF BEAUTIFUL WRITING *Katherine Jeffares*   7.00
____ CALLIGRAPHY FOR FUN & PROFIT *Anne Leptich & Jacque Evans*   7.00
____ CALLIGRAPHY MADE EASY *Tina Serafini*   7.00

CHESS & CHECKERS
____ BEGINNER'S GUIDE TO WINNING CHESS *Fred Reinfeld*   5.00
____ CHESS IN TEN EASY LESSONS *Larry Evans*   5.00
____ CHESS MADE EASY *Milton L. Hanauer*   5.00
____ CHESS PROBLEMS FOR BEGINNERS *Edited by Fred Reinfeld*   5.00
____ CHESS TACTICS FOR BEGINNERS *Edited by Fred Reinfeld*   5.00
____ CHESS THEORY & PRACTICE *Morry & Mitchell*   2.00

____ HOW TO WIN AT CHECKERS *Fred Reinfeld*		5.00
____ 1001 BRILLIANT WAYS TO CHECKMATE *Fred Reinfeld*		7.00
____ 1001 WINNING CHESS SACRIFICES & COMBINATIONS *Fred Reinfeld*		7.00

COOKERY & HERBS

____ CULPEPER'S HERBAL REMEDIES *Dr. Nicholas Culpeper*		5.00
____ FAST GOURMET COOKBOOK *Poppy Cannon*		2.50
____ HEALING POWER OF HERBS *May Bethel*		5.00
____ HEALING POWER OF NATURAL FOODS *May Bethel*		5.00
____ HERBS FOR HEALTH—HOW TO GROW & USE THEM *Louise Evans Doole*		4.00
____ HOME GARDEN COOKBOOK—DELICIOUS NATURAL FOOD RECIPES *Ken Kraft*		3.00
____ MEATLESS MEAL GUIDE *Tomi Ryan & James H. Ryan, M.D.*		4.00
____ VEGETABLE GARDENING FOR BEGINNERS *Hugh Wiberg*		2.00
____ VEGETABLES FOR TODAY'S GARDENS *R. Milton Carleton*		2.00
____ VEGETARIAN COOKERY *Janet Walker*		7.00
____ VEGETARIAN COOKING MADE EASY & DELECTABLE *Veronica Vezza*		3.00
____ VEGETARIAN DELIGHTS—A HAPPY COOKBOOK FOR HEALTH *K. R. Mehta*		2.00
____ VEGETARIAN GOURMET COOKBOOK *Joyce McKinnel*		3.00

GAMBLING & POKER

____ ADVANCED POKER STRATEGY & WINNING PLAY *A. D. Livingston*		5.00
____ HOW TO WIN AT DICE GAMES *Skip Frey*		3.00
____ HOW TO WIN AT POKER *Terence Reese & Anthony T. Watkins*		5.00
____ WINNING AT CRAPS *Dr. Lloyd T. Commins*		5.00
____ WINNING AT GIN *Chester Wander & Cy Rice*		3.00
____ WINNING AT POKER—AN EXPERT'S GUIDE *John Archer*		5.00
____ WINNING AT 21—AN EXPERT'S GUIDE *John Archer*		5.00
____ WINNING POKER SYSTEMS *Norman Zadeh*		3.00

HEALTH

____ BEE POLLEN *Lynda Lyngheim & Jack Scagnetti*		3.00
____ COPING WITH ALZHEIMER'S *Rose Oliver, Ph.D. & Francis Bock, Ph.D.*		7.00
____ DR. LINDNER'S POINT SYSTEM FOOD PROGRAM *Peter G. Lindner, M.D.*		2.00
____ HELP YOURSELF TO BETTER SIGHT *Margaret Darst Corbett*		7.00
____ HOW YOU CAN STOP SMOKING PERMANENTLY *Ernest Caldwell*		5.00
____ MIND OVER PLATTER *Peter G. Lindner, M.D.*		5.00
____ NATURE'S WAY TO NUTRITION & VIBRANT HEALTH *Robert J. Scrutton*		3.00
____ NEW CARBOHYDRATE DIET COUNTER *Patti Lopez-Pereira*		2.00
____ REFLEXOLOGY *Dr. Maybelle Segal*		4.00
____ REFLEXOLOGY FOR GOOD HEALTH *Anna Kaye & Don C. Matchan*		5.00
____ 30 DAYS TO BEAUTIFUL LEGS *Dr. Marc Selner*		3.00
____ YOU CAN LEARN TO RELAX *Dr. Samuel Gutwirth*		3.00

HOBBIES

____ BEACHCOMBING FOR BEGINNERS *Norman Hickin*		2.00
____ BLACKSTONE'S MODERN CARD TRICKS *Harry Blackstone*		5.00
____ BLACKSTONE'S SECRETS OF MAGIC *Harry Blackstone*		5.00
____ COIN COLLECTING FOR BEGINNERS *Burton Hobson & Fred Reinfeld*		5.00
____ ENTERTAINING WITH ESP *Tony 'Doc' Shiels*		2.00
____ 400 FASCINATING MAGIC TRICKS YOU CAN DO *Howard Thurston*		5.00
____ HOW I TURN JUNK INTO FUN AND PROFIT *Sari*		3.00
____ HOW TO WRITE A HIT SONG & SELL IT *Tommy Boyce*		7.00
____ JUGGLING MADE EASY *Rudolf Dittrich*		3.00
____ MAGIC FOR ALL AGES *Walter Gibson*		4.00
____ MAGIC MADE EASY *Byron Wels*		2.00
____ STAMP COLLECTING FOR BEGINNERS *Burton Hobson*		3.00

HORSE PLAYER'S WINNING GUIDES

____ BETTING HORSES TO WIN *Les Conklin*		5.00
____ ELIMINATE THE LOSERS *Bob McKnight*		5.00
____ HOW TO PICK WINNING HORSES *Bob McKnight*		5.00

____ HOW TO WIN AT THE RACES *Sam (The Genius) Lewin*		5.00
____ HOW YOU CAN BEAT THE RACES *Jack Kavanagh*		5.00
____ MAKING MONEY AT THE RACES *David Barr*		5.00
____ PAYDAY AT THE RACES *Les Conklin*		5.00
____ SMART HANDICAPPING MADE EASY *William Bauman*		5.00
____ SUCCESS AT THE HARNESS RACES *Barry Meadow*		5.00
____ WINNING AT THE HARNESS RACES—AN EXPERT'S GUIDE *Nick Cammarano*		5.00

HUMOR

____ HOW TO FLATTEN YOUR TUSH *Coach Marge Reardon*		2.00
____ HOW TO MAKE LOVE TO YOURSELF *Ron Stevens & Joy Grdnic*		3.00
____ JOKE TELLER'S HANDBOOK *Bob Orben*		7.00
____ JOKES FOR ALL OCCASIONS *Al Schock*		5.00
____ 2,000 NEW LAUGHS FOR SPEAKERS *Bob Orben*		5.00
____ 2,400 JOKES TO BRIGHTEN YOUR SPEECHES *Robert Orben*		7.00
____ 2,500 JOKES TO START 'EM LAUGHING *Bob Orben*		7.00

HYPNOTISM

____ ADVANCED TECHNIQUES OF HYPNOSIS *Melvin Powers*		3.00
____ CHILDBIRTH WITH HYPNOSIS *William S. Kroger, M.D.*		5.00
____ HOW TO SOLVE YOUR SEX PROBLEMS WITH SELF-HYPNOSIS *Frank S. Caprio, M.D.*		5.00
____ HOW TO STOP SMOKING THRU SELF-HYPNOSIS *Leslie M. LeCron*		3.00
____ HOW TO USE AUTO-SUGGESTION EFFECTIVELY *John Duckworth*		3.00
____ HOW YOU CAN BOWL BETTER USING SELF-HYPNOSIS *Jack Heise*		4.00
____ HOW YOU CAN PLAY BETTER GOLF USING SELF-HYPNOSIS *Jack Heise*		3.00
____ HYPNOSIS AND SELF-HYPNOSIS *Bernard Hollander, M.D.*		5.00
____ HYPNOTISM *(Originally published in 1893) Carl Sextus*		5.00
____ HYPNOTISM & PSYCHIC PHENOMENA *Simeon Edmunds*		4.00
____ HYPNOTISM MADE EASY *Dr. Ralph Winn*		5.00
____ HYPNOTISM MADE PRACTICAL *Louis Orton*		5.00
____ HYPNOTISM REVEALED *Melvin Powers*		3.00
____ HYPNOTISM TODAY *Leslie LeCron and Jean Bordeaux, Ph.D.*		5.00
____ MODERN HYPNOSIS *Lesley Kuhn & Salvatore Russo, Ph.D.*		5.00
____ NEW CONCEPTS OF HYPNOSIS *Bernard C. Gindes, M.D.*		7.00
____ NEW SELF-HYPNOSIS *Paul Adams*		7.00
____ POST-HYPNOTIC INSTRUCTIONS—SUGGESTIONS FOR THERAPY *Arnold Furst*		5.00
____ PRACTICAL GUIDE TO SELF-HYPNOSIS *Melvin Powers*		3.00
____ PRACTICAL HYPNOTISM *Philip Magonet, M.D.*		3.00
____ SECRETS OF HYPNOTISM *S. J. Van Pelt, M.D.*		5.00
____ SELF-HYPNOSIS—A CONDITIONED-RESPONSE TECHNIQUE *Laurence Sparks*		7.00
____ SELF-HYPNOSIS—ITS THEORY, TECHNIQUE & APPLICATION *Melvin Powers*		3.00
____ THERAPY THROUGH HYPNOSIS *Edited by Raphael H. Rhodes*		5.00

JUDAICA

____ SERVICE OF THE HEART *Evelyn Garfiel, Ph.D.*		7.00
____ STORY OF ISRAEL IN COINS *Jean & Maurice Gould*		2.00
____ STORY OF ISRAEL IN STAMPS *Maxim & Gabriel Shamir*		1.00
____ TONGUE OF THE PROPHETS *Robert St. John*		7.00

JUST FOR WOMEN

____ COSMOPOLITAN'S GUIDE TO MARVELOUS MEN Foreword by *Helen Gurley Brown*		3.00
____ COSMOPOLITAN'S HANG-UP HANDBOOK Foreword by *Helen Gurley Brown*		4.00
____ COSMOPOLITAN'S LOVE BOOK—A GUIDE TO ECSTASY IN BED		7.00
____ COSMOPOLITAN'S NEW ETIQUETTE GUIDE Foreword by *Helen Gurley Brown*		4.00
____ I AM A COMPLEAT WOMAN *Doris Hagopian & Karen O'Connor Sweeney*		3.00
____ JUST FOR WOMEN—A GUIDE TO THE FEMALE BODY *Richard E. Sand, M.D.*		5.00
____ NEW APPROACHES TO SEX IN MARRIAGE *John E. Eichenlaub, M.D.*		3.00
____ SEXUALLY ADEQUATE FEMALE *Frank S. Caprio, M.D.*		3.00
____ SEXUALLY FULFILLED WOMAN *Dr. Rachel Copelan*		5.00
____ YOUR FIRST YEAR OF MARRIAGE *Dr. Tom McGinnis*		3.00

MARRIAGE, SEX & PARENTHOOD

____ ABILITY TO LOVE *Dr. Allan Fromme*		7.00

____ GUIDE TO SUCCESSFUL MARRIAGE Drs. Albert Ellis & Robert Harper		7.00
____ HOW TO RAISE AN EMOTIONALLY HEALTHY, HAPPY CHILD Albert Ellis, Ph.D.		7.00
____ PARENT SURVIVAL TRAINING Marvin Silverman, Ed.D. & David Lustig, Ph.D.		10.00
____ SEX WITHOUT GUILT Albert Ellis, Ph.D.		5.00
____ SEXUALLY ADEQUATE MALE Frank S. Caprio, M.D.		3.00
____ SEXUALLY FULFILLED MAN Dr. Rachel Copelan		5.00
____ STAYING IN LOVE Dr. Norton F. Kristy		7.00

MELVIN POWERS' MAIL ORDER LIBRARY

____ HOW TO GET RICH IN MAIL ORDER Melvin Powers		20.00
____ HOW TO WRITE A GOOD ADVERTISEMENT Victor O. Schwab		20.00
____ MAIL ORDER MADE EASY J. Frank Brumbaugh		20.00

METAPHYSICS & OCCULT

____ BOOK OF TALISMANS, AMULETS & ZODIACAL GEMS William Pavitt		7.00
____ CONCENTRATION—A GUIDE TO MENTAL MASTERY Mouni Sadhu		7.00
____ EXTRA-TERRESTRIAL INTELLIGENCE—THE FIRST ENCOUNTER		6.00
____ FORTUNE TELLING WITH CARDS P. Foli		5.00
____ HOW TO INTERPRET DREAMS, OMENS & FORTUNE TELLING SIGNS Gettings		5.00
____ HOW TO UNDERSTAND YOUR DREAMS Geoffrey A. Dudley		5.00
____ IN DAYS OF GREAT PEACE Mouni Sadhu		3.00
____ MAGICIAN—HIS TRAINING AND WORK W. E. Butler		5.00
____ MEDITATION Mouni Sadhu		7.00
____ MODERN NUMEROLOGY Morris C. Goodman		5.00
____ NUMEROLOGY—ITS FACTS AND SECRETS Ariel Yvon Taylor		5.00
____ NUMEROLOGY MADE EASY W. Mykian		5.00
____ PALMISTRY MADE EASY Fred Gettings		5.00
____ PALMISTRY MADE PRACTICAL Elizabeth Daniels Squire		5.00
____ PALMISTRY SECRETS REVEALED Henry Frith		4.00
____ PROPHECY IN OUR TIME Martin Ebon		2.50
____ SUPERSTITION—ARE YOU SUPERSTITIOUS? Eric Maple		2.00
____ TAROT Mouni Sadhu		10.00
____ TAROT OF THE BOHEMIANS Papus		7.00
____ WAYS TO SELF-REALIZATION Mouni Sadhu		7.00
____ WITCHCRAFT, MAGIC & OCCULTISM—A FASCINATING HISTORY W. B. Crow		7.00
____ WITCHCRAFT—THE SIXTH SENSE Justine Glass		7.00
____ WORLD OF PSYCHIC RESEARCH Hereward Carrington		2.00

SELF-HELP & INSPIRATIONAL

____ CHARISMA—HOW TO GET "THAT SPECIAL MAGIC" Marcia Grad		7.00
____ DAILY POWER FOR JOYFUL LIVING Dr. Donald Curtis		7.00
____ DYNAMIC THINKING Melvin Powers		5.00
____ GREATEST POWER IN THE UNIVERSE U. S. Andersen		7.00
____ GROW RICH WHILE YOU SLEEP Ben Sweetland		7.00
____ GROWTH THROUGH REASON Albert Ellis, Ph.D.		7.00
____ GUIDE TO PERSONAL HAPPINESS Albert Ellis, Ph.D. & Irving Becker, Ed.D.		7.00
____ HANDWRITING ANALYSIS MADE EASY John Marley		7.00
____ HANDWRITING TELLS Nadya Olyanova		7.00
____ HOW TO ATTRACT GOOD LUCK A.H.Z. Carr		7.00
____ HOW TO BE GREAT Dr. Donald Curtis		5.00
____ HOW TO DEVELOP A WINNING PERSONALITY Martin Panzer		5.00
____ HOW TO DEVELOP AN EXCEPTIONAL MEMORY Young & Gibson		5.00
____ HOW TO LIVE WITH A NEUROTIC Albert Ellis, Ph.D.		7.00
____ HOW TO OVERCOME YOUR FEARS M. P. Leahy, M.D.		3.00
____ HOW TO SUCCEED Brian Adams		7.00
____ HUMAN PROBLEMS & HOW TO SOLVE THEM Dr. Donald Curtis		5.00
____ I CAN Ben Sweetland		7.00
____ I WILL Ben Sweetland		3.00
____ KNIGHT IN THE RUSTY ARMOR Robert Fisher		5.00

____ LEFT-HANDED PEOPLE *Michael Barsley*		5.00
____ MAGIC IN YOUR MIND *U.S. Andersen*		7.00
____ MAGIC OF THINKING BIG *Dr. David J. Schwartz*		3.00
____ MAGIC OF THINKING SUCCESS *Dr. David J. Schwartz*		7.00
____ MAGIC POWER OF YOUR MIND *Walter M. Germain*		7.00
____ MENTAL POWER THROUGH SLEEP SUGGESTION *Melvin Powers*		3.00
____ NEVER UNDERESTIMATE THE SELLING POWER OF A WOMAN *Dottie Walters*		7.00
____ NEW GUIDE TO RATIONAL LIVING *Albert Ellis, Ph.D. & R. Harper, Ph.D.*		7.00
____ PSYCHO-CYBERNETICS *Maxwell Maltz, M.D.*		7.00
____ PSYCHOLOGY OF HANDWRITING *Nadya Olyanova*		7.00
____ SALES CYBERNETICS *Brian Adams*		7.00
____ SCIENCE OF MIND IN DAILY LIVING *Dr. Donald Curtis*		7.00
____ SECRET OF SECRETS *U.S. Andersen*		7.00
____ SECRET POWER OF THE PYRAMIDS *U. S. Andersen*		7.00
____ SELF-THERAPY FOR THE STUTTERER *Malcolm Frazer*		3.00
____ SUCCESS-CYBERNETICS *U. S. Andersen*		7.00
____ 10 DAYS TO A GREAT NEW LIFE *William E. Edwards*		3.00
____ THINK AND GROW RICH *Napoleon Hill*		7.00
____ THREE MAGIC WORDS *U. S. Andersen*		7.00
____ TREASURY OF COMFORT *Edited by Rabbi Sidney Greenberg*		7.00
____ TREASURY OF THE ART OF LIVING *Sidney S. Greenberg*		7.00
____ WHAT YOUR HANDWRITING REVEALS *Albert E. Hughes*		4.00
____ YOUR SUBCONSCIOUS POWER *Charles M. Simmons*		7.00
____ YOUR THOUGHTS CAN CHANGE YOUR LIFE *Dr. Donald Curtis*		7.00

SPORTS

____ BICYCLING FOR FUN AND GOOD HEALTH *Kenneth E. Luther*		2.00
____ BILLIARDS—POCKET • CAROM • THREE CUSHION *Clive Cottingham, Jr.*		5.00
____ COMPLETE GUIDE TO FISHING *Vlad Evanoff*		2.00
____ HOW TO IMPROVE YOUR RACQUETBALL *Lubarsky, Kaufman & Scagnetti*		5.00
____ HOW TO WIN AT POCKET BILLIARDS *Edward D. Knuchell*		7.00
____ JOY OF WALKING *Jack Scagnetti*		3.00
____ LEARNING & TEACHING SOCCER SKILLS *Eric Worthington*		3.00
____ MOTORCYCLING FOR BEGINNERS *I.G. Edmonds*		3.00
____ RACQUETBALL FOR WOMEN *Toni Hudson, Jack Scagnetti & Vince Rondone*		3.00
____ RACQUETBALL MADE EASY *Steve Lubarsky, Rod Delson & Jack Scagnetti*		5.00
____ SECRET OF BOWLING STRIKES *Dawson Taylor*		5.00
____ SECRET OF PERFECT PUTTING *Horton Smith & Dawson Taylor*		5.00
____ SOCCER—THE GAME & HOW TO PLAY IT *Gary Rosenthal*		5.00
____ STARTING SOCCER *Edward F. Dolan, Jr.*		5.00

TENNIS LOVER'S LIBRARY

____ BEGINNER'S GUIDE TO WINNING TENNIS *Helen Hull Jacobs*		2.00
____ HOW TO BEAT BETTER TENNIS PLAYERS *Loring Fiske*		4.00
____ PSYCH YOURSELF TO BETTER TENNIS *Dr. Walter A. Luszki*		2.00
____ TENNIS FOR BEGINNERS *Dr. H. A. Murray*		2.00
____ TENNIS MADE EASY *Joel Brecheen*		5.00
____ WEEKEND TENNIS—HOW TO HAVE FUN & WIN AT THE SAME TIME *Bill Talbert*		3.00
____ WINNING WITH PERCENTAGE TENNIS—SMART STRATEGY *Jack Lowe*		2.00

WILSHIRE PET LIBRARY

____ DOG OBEDIENCE TRAINING *Gust Kessopulos*		5.00
____ DOG TRAINING MADE EASY & FUN *John W. Kellogg*		5.00
____ HOW TO BRING UP YOUR PET DOG *Kurt Unkelbach*		2.00
____ HOW TO RAISE & TRAIN YOUR PUPPY *Jeff Griffen*		5.00

The books listed above can be obtained from your book dealer or directly from Melvin Powers. When ordering, please remit $1.50 postage for the first book and 50¢ for each additional book.

Melvin Powers
12015 Sherman Road, No. Hollywood, California 91605